POCKET GUIDE TO
Spanish for the Nutrition Professional

THIRD EDITION

Peggy Durbala

MA

Mary Jo Kurko

MPH, RD, LDN, CPXP

Academy of Nutrition and Dietetics
Chicago, IL

eat right. Academy of Nutrition and Dietetics

Academy of Nutrition and Dietetics
120 S. Riverside Plaza, Suite 2190
Chicago, IL 60606

Academy of Nutrition and Dietetics Pocket Guide to Spanish for the Nutrition Professional,
Third Edition

ISBN 978-0-88091-944-9 (print)
ISBN 978-0-88091-945-6 (eBook)
Catalog Number 406819 (print)
Catalog Number 406819e (eBook)

10   9   8   7   6   5   4   3   2   1

For more information on the Academy of Nutrition and Dietetics, visit www.eatright.org.

Library of Congress Cataloging-in-Publication Data

Names: Durbala, Peggy author. | Kurko, Mary Jo, author.
Title: Academy of nutrition and dietetics pocket guide to Spanish for the
  nutrition professional / Peggy Durbala, Mary Jo Kurko.
Other titles: Spanish for the nutrition professional
Description: Third edition. | Chicago, IL : Academy of Nutrition and
  Dietetics, 2018. | Originally published: Chicago, Ill. : American Dietetic
  Association, c2005, under title: Spanish for the nutrition professional /
  Peggy A. Batty. | Includes bibliographical references and index.
Identifiers: LCCN 2018001847 | ISBN 9780880919449 (print)
Subjects: LCSH: Spanish language--Conversation and phrase books (for
  nutritionists)
Classification: LCC PC4120.N87 B38 2018 | DDC 468.3/4210246132--dc23 LC record available at https://lccn.loc.gov/2018001847

Contents

Contents

Section III: Nutrition Care Education and Resources

Reviewers

Sandra Arevalo, MPH, RDN, CDN, CDE, CLC, FADA
Director of Nutrition and Outreach Services
South Bronx Health Center
Bronx, NY

Melissa Baugh, RD, CD
Clinical Dietitian
Utah State Hospital and Intermountain Healthcare
Provo, UT

Denisse Porras Fimbres, RDN, LD
Clinical Dietitian
Emory Healthcare
Decatur, GA

Sylvia E. Klinger, DBA, MS, RDN
Nutrition and Culinary Consultant
Hispanic Food Communications, Inc.
Hinsdale, IL

Lisa Schnepp, RD, CDE
Clinical Nutrition Services Manager,
Diabetes Educator
Major Hospital/Major Hospital Partners
Indianapolis, IN

Maria Virginia Tijerina Walls, MS, PhD candidate,
NC Director, Professor, and Researcher
Nutrien Nutrición y Salud
Autonomous University of Nuevo León
San Pedro Garza García, Nuevo León, Mexico

Foreword

In the profession of dietetics, we speak of competencies and level of proficiency. While I am proficient in many domains in dietetics, when it comes to the ability to communicate with Hispanic and Latino clients or colleagues, I am definitely a novice. A few greetings, simple phrases, and requesting expense accounts in Spanish (which I learned when I was LAHIDAN Treasurer) encompass my bilingual skills.

Tools like the *Academy of Nutrition and Dietetics Pocket Guide to Spanish for the Nutrition Professional*, Third Edition, are invaluable resources for dietetics practitioners to provide culturally sensitive nutrition care for their Spanish-speaking clients. This concise and straightforward guide enables anyone to become more comfortable with conversational Spanish related to food, nutrition, eating, and health and be more aware of Hispanic/Latino culture. The third edition of the *Academy of Nutrition and Dietetics Pocket Guide to Spanish for the Nutrition Professional* promises to be an excellent resource, much like previous editions. This new edition presents additional words, phrases, and updated evidence-based material related to culture and counseling. Central American foods and cultural components have also been added. The three sections, Section I: Culturally Sensitive Nutrition Care of Spanish-speaking clients, Section II: Spanish Grammar and Vocabulary for the Nutrition Professional, and Section III: Nutrition Care Education and Resources provide the user with invaluable and comprehensive information to help practitioners assess the individual's food and nutrition needs and beliefs. The third edition comes with downloadable food cards with Spanish pronunciation and standard serving sizes to use as a visual aid in counseling and can also be used for practitioners to practice their Spanish skills. A diagram showing the names and pronunciation key for body parts has been expanded to include more body parts and organs.

This book is a service to the members of the Academy as well as other health care providers. Anyone looking for an accurate and thorough text on the Hispanic/Latino culture and how to communicate effectively in Spanish will find this handbook a key tool in their care of the Spanish-speaking client.

Margaret Cook-Newell PhD, RDN, LD, CN

*Chair, Latinos and Hispanics in Dietetics and Nutrition (LAHIDAN)
A Member Interest Group of the Academy of Nutrition and Dietetics*

LAHIDAN Board of Directors 2017-2018

Chair: Margaret Cook-Newell, PhD, RDN, LD, CN

Chair-Elect: Sara Carrión Perrone, MS, RDN, LD

Secretary: Magaly Hernandez, MPH, RDN, LDN

Treasurer: Nathan Myers, MS, RD, CDN

Immediate Past Chair: Diana Romano, MS, RD, LD

Nominating Committee Chair: Crystal Rivero Young, RDN

Nominating Chair-Elect: Virginia Tijerina Walls, MS, NC

Mentoring Coordinator: Julie Plasencia, PhD, RDN

Acknowledgments

I would like to thank Beth Vinkler, Julie Moreschi, Julie Davis, Catherine Arnold, and Becky Iacopetti of Benedictine University for their help and encouragement with this project; all the students who have taken the Spanish for Nutrition Professionals course and contributed their ideas; and my daughters, Tara and Robin, for helping me put my original book together.

I would also especially like to thank Mary Jo Kurko for collaborating with me to bring this publication to fruition and my husband, Matt Durbala, for his support and encouragement of me in this endeavor and so many others.

Peggy A. Batty-Durbala, MA

Since the first edition of *Spanish for the Nutrition Professional*, I've been gratified to see the increase in interest and research in health literacy, cultural competence, and new techniques in interviewing and counseling. I appreciate the opportunity to contribute to this valuable resource and to renew my friendship with Peggy

Batty-Durbala in the process. Thanks to the Academy of Nutrition and Dietetics for seeing the value in revising and improving the book.

I would also like to thank my daughters, Maggie and Annie, who continue to support me with this and many other projects. Thanks, too, to my wonderful, bilingual grandchildren, Nicholas and Zoe, whose Spanish "lessons" have taught me more than any academic course.

Mary Jo Kurko, MPH, RD, LDN, CPXP

Section I

Culturally Sensitive Nutrition Care of Spanish-Speaking Clients

CHAPTER 1

Latino Culture

Hispanic/Latino Diversity

The term *Hispanic* is an ethnic category that denotes neither race nor color. Although the term is widely used, many members of the Hispanic population prefer the term *Latino*. The US Census Bureau considers the terms interchangeable; the 2010 census categories of Hispanic origins listed Mexican, Mexican-American, Chicano; Puerto Rican; Cuban; and Other.[1]

Despite the common use of the Spanish language and cultural similarities, there is tremendous variety within the Latino community. Latinos in the United States are stereotypically thought of as Mexicans (in California, Texas, Illinois, and Arizona), as Puerto Ricans (in New York, New Jersey, and the East Coast), or as Cubans (in Florida). However, the community also includes people from the Caribbean, Central America, South America, as well as individuals in the Southwest who were born in the United States but whose ancestors were Spanish.[2]

According to the Census Bureau, as of July 1, 2015, Hispanics/Latinos comprise about 17.6% (56.6 million individuals) of the US population. Latinos are the largest minority group in the United States, and the population is expected to increase to 28.6% (119 million) by 2060.[2] Because only 4% of the dietetics profession identifies as Hispanic/Latino, counseling Latino clients can be a challenge for nutrition and dietetics professionals.[3] Most registered dietitian nutritionists will be counseling members of a cultural group that differs from their own.

Basic Cultural Factors

Cultural competency is an essential skill for nutrition professionals. To provide appropriate care to Latino clients, nutrition and dietetics professionals must first understand Latino culture. Although there are differences among these cultures, similarities include the Spanish language, importance of family, and religious faith.[4]

The Latino family may include parents, their children, grandparents, cousins, aunts and uncles, godparents, and close family friends. The father is often the "head of the family," and the mother is usually responsible for the home. Family members feel responsibility for one another, especially for those with health problems. Therefore, it is not unusual for family members to accompany the client to nutrition counseling. If this is the case, keep in mind that it is common for the father to make health decisions for other family members.[5]

Religion may be another factor for the nutrition professional to consider in the decision-making process. The church is often part of daily family and community life (many Latinos are Catholic) and plays an even greater role in times of illness.[5]

Although most Latinos speak Spanish, there are numerous dialects used within the community. Individuals from different countries (or different areas of the same country) may not share the same meaning of a particular word. Some immigrants, especially those from parts of Mexico and Central America, may speak a native language other than Spanish. Despite the differences in vocabulary, most Spanish-speaking Latinos have no difficulty conversing with each other. Young people who have been raised in the United States commonly use a mix of Spanish and English.

Difficulty in accessing and using the health care system in the United States is a significant problem for many Latinos, especially those of lower socioeconomic status. Language barriers, a low rate of medical insurance coverage, the lack of transportation to and from clinics and hospitals, and low incomes are just a few factors that contribute to difficulty in accessing services.[6]

Potential Differences Among Cultural Groups

Nutrition professionals should consider potential differences among cultural groups when conducting a cross-cultural counseling session. These differences include:

- **Socioeconomic and environmental factors** Socioeconomic issues (including legal status) and environmental risks can affect health and treatment and influence a client's attitudes, beliefs, and values.

- **Language** New immigrants are likely to speak only Spanish. Furthermore, many Latinos who speak and understand spoken English cannot read or write that language. Parents who cannot speak English may ask their children to translate; however, this is not appropriate in medical discussions. A trained interpreter should be used (see Chapter 4).

- **Family structure and social values** Western medicine makes an individual responsible for his or her health care. The Latino culture of extended family invites collective decision making, which is likely to involve the head of the household. Strong traditional gender roles (eg, the mother is responsible for cooking and feeding the family) may lead women to perceive the changes suggested in nutrition counseling negatively.

- **Cultural food practices** Food behaviors that are reflective of the Latino culture (such as food preferences, food preparation, eating patterns, and foods used as medicine or to promote health) are most evident in recent immigrants, but some cultural behaviors persist for generations.

- **Health care values, beliefs, and practices** Although Western cultures rely on science to explain illness and treat disease, some members of different Latino cultures focus on the spiritual causes of illness.

- **Attitudes toward health care providers** Some Latinos (especially men) may feel that seeking medical attention is a sign of weakness. They may solicit a health care provider's assistance only after a disease has progressed—not for preventive care or natural processes like pregnancy. Also, some Latinos may use home remedies for an illness before visiting a physician and they may be more likely to follow the advice of a relative or neighbor than a health professional.[6,7]

- **Nutrition professional designation** The vocabulary for nutrition professionals varies by country or region. In this book, the registered dietitian nutritionist (RDN) title is referred to as Nutricionista. However, other terms may be used elsewhere, for example, Dietista Nutricionista Registrado, Nutriólogo (commonly used in Mexico), Nutricionista–Dietista Registrada (used in Columbia), or Dietista (in Mexico, this term refers to dietetic technician).

References

1. Humes KR, Jones NA, Ramirez RR. Overview of race and His-
    panic Origin: 2010. US Census Bureau 2010 Census Briefs.
    www.census.gov/content/dam/Census/library/publications
    /2011/dec/c2010br-02.pdf. Accessed June 19, 2017.

2. US Census Bureau. Facts for features: Hispanic Heritage
    Month 2016. www.census.gov/newsroom/facts-for-features
    /2016/cb16-ff16.html. Accessed July 19, 2017.

3. Academy of Nutrition and Dietetics. *Compensation and Bene-
    fits Survey of the Dietetics Profession 2015*. Chicago, IL: Academy
    of Nutrition and Dietetics; 2016.

4. Kittler PG, Sucher KP, Nahikian-Nelms M. *Food and Culture*.
    7th ed. Boston, MA: Cengage Learning; 2017.

5. Medina C. Belief and Traditions that impact the Latino
    healthcare. www.medschool.lsuhsc.edu/physiology/docs
    /Belief%20and%20Traditions%20that%20impact%20the%20
    Latino%20Healthcare.pdf. Accessed May 17, 2017.

6. Juckett G. Caring for Latino patients. *Am Fam Physician*.
    2013;87:48-54.

7. Boyle M. *Community Nutrition in Action: An Entrepreneurial
    Approach*. 7th ed. Boston, MA: Cengage Learning; 2017.

Nutrition Care

CHAPTER 2

Folk Beliefs, Lay Healers, and Other Treatments in Latino Cultures

Although some Latinos may use folk or home remedies to treat illness, they likely also use (sometimes simultaneously) antibiotics and other medications. Furthermore, some Latinos may believe that health in general is a matter of fate and so may feel little responsibility for seeking treatment.[1,2]

To provide appropriate counseling, the nutrition professional must understand the client's cultural beliefs. In fact, what may be most important to Latino clients is not education and training but the manner in which nutrition counseling is provided.

Latinos of Mexican and Puerto Rican descent may subscribe to two folk beliefs that could have nutritional implications: the hot/cold theory and soul loss.

Hot/Cold Theory

In this theory, balancing hot and cold is a component of maintaining good health.[1] The properties "hot" and "cold" are assigned to foods and conditions, but not everyone assigns these properties in the same way. Generally, hot conditions are related to vasodilation and high metabolic rate. For example, pregnancy, hypertension, diabetes, acid reflux, and *susto* (soul loss) are usually considered hot conditions. On the other hand, cold conditions involve vasoconstriction and low metabolic rate. Examples might include headache, earache, or cramps.[1]

Based on the hot/cold theory, a hot condition would require a cold food to restore balance, whereas a cold condition calls for hot herbs and foods. Chili peppers, garlic, onion, most grains, and tuna are examples of hot foods, whereas cold foods usually include vegetables, tropical fruits, dairy products, and white fish. Beans and food made of corn, rice, or wheat, as well as foods high in sugar, are deemed hot or cold depending on how they are prepared.[2]

Keep in mind that Latinos who follow folk beliefs, such as the hot/cold theory, may avoid sharing that with health care providers.[1,2] Use careful, indirect questions to find out whether your client believes in such theories. Indirect questions start with words like "could you tell me" or "I was wondering." For example, the question, "I was wondering if you have tried any herbal or food remedies?" could lead into a discussion about the hot/cold theory.[3]

Working with your client's individual food beliefs will increase satisfaction and compliance with the nutrition care plan.

Soul Loss

Susto, or soul loss, is an ailment believed to be caused by excessive emotion. It is considered a serious condition associated with a number of diseases, including cancer, kidney failure, diabetes, and high blood pressure. Symptoms can include anxiety, depression or sadness, lack of appetite, paleness, shaking, headaches, and ennui.[2] This belief in soul loss can explain a Latino client's reluctance to consult health care providers.[1,2] As with the hot/cold theory, knowing if your client subscribes to a belief in *susto* can help you develop a culturally appropriate nutrition care plan.

Lay Healers

The initial treatment for some Latino clients might be a home remedy, such as a tea made from various herbs or spices. If home remedies are ineffective, advice from a *yerbero* (herbalist) or a *sobador* (massage therapist) could be sought.[2] If the advice is also ineffective, the next step could be to consult a *curandero* (lay healer). Through a combination of spiritualistic practices and Western medicine, the *curandero* seeks to treat the physical and psychological aspects of illness. Lay healers are most often used by first-generation immigrants.[1]

Latinos are far more likely to use physicians as primary sources of health care than they are to use lay healers. However, a client may simultaneously use prayer, folk and herbal remedies, and prescription medications.

Herbal Remedies and Other Treatments

Herbs are used for disease treatment in many cultures. Many herbal remedies are harmless, and there is evidence of efficacy for some. However, ingredients in herbal preparations may interact with medications, and some herbal remedies are dangerous.[1,2] When working with any client, the nutrition professional should seek to determine if herbal remedies are being used.

Commonly used herbs that are safe for most clients include: garlic (for oral yeast infections or toothache pain; however, large doses are contraindicated in clients taking warfarin); oregano (for fever and dry cough);

chamomile (for colic, menstrual cramps, and insomnia); boiled peanut broth (for diarrhea); eucalyptus (in a vaporizer for bronchitis; however, eucalyptus oil should not be taken internally); peppermint (for dyspepsia); and aloe vera (for burns).[2]

Unsafe treatments include *azarcón* and *greta*, which are lead- and mercury-based products that may be used for gastrointestinal conditions. The traditional honey-and-water remedy for infant colic should be avoided because of the risk of botulism associated with honey.[2] Because many herbs interact with medications, consult a pharmacist or a reputable herbal text for guidance if your client is taking a specific herb or giving it to a young child. Sources often disagree on the safety of herbs; however, there is some consensus that aconite, chaparral, comfrey, germander, kava, lobelia, and pennyroyal are unsafe.[4,5]

References

1. Juckett G. Caring for Latino patients. *Am Fam Physician*. 2013;87:48-54.

2. Kittler PG, Sucher KP, Nahikian-Nelms M. *Food and Culture*. 7th ed. Boston, MA: Cengage Learning; 2017.

3. Espresso English. Direct and indirect questions in English. www.espressoenglish.net/direct-and-indirect-questions-in-english. Accessed October 10, 2017.

4. Consumer Reports. 15 supplement ingredients to always avoid. www.consumerreports.org/vitamins-supplements/15-supplement-ingredients-to-always-avoid. Accessed May 17, 2017.

5. Collins S. 5 risky herbal supplements. www.webmd.com/vitamins-and-supplements/features/risky-herbal-supplements#1. Accessed May 5, 2017.

CHAPTER 3

Differences in Dietary Habits Within the Latino Community

Latino Dietary Habits and Staple Foods

To provide appropriate counseling, the nutrition professional must have a knowledge and understanding of the client's culture and ethnic food practices. An understanding of the factors that impact a client's decision-making process provides the professional an opportunity to implement permanent behavior change rather than simply prescribing a diet.[1]

Some general nutrition concerns for Latino clients include[2,3]:

- high fat intake (sometimes in the form of lard), which may offset the benefits of a diet high in vegetable protein and carbohydrates from beans and rice or beans and corn;
- few servings of milk and green or leafy vegetables;
- diet high in sugar, including sweetened beverages; and
- increased incorporation of fast food in the diet as acculturation occurs.

In many Spanish-speaking countries, a light meal is served for *desayuno* (breakfast). The main meal of the day is *almuerzo, comida,* or *lonche* (lunch). *La merienda*, *bocadillos*, or *entrecomidas* is a light snack (mostly for children), which may be served in the late afternoon or early evening. In the late evening, a *cena* or *comida* (small supper) is eaten.[3] As acculturation occurs, most Latinos adopt the 3-meals-a-day pattern (with the heavier meal in the evening).

Although food preparation and practices can change slowly for Latinos once they arrive in the United States, some practices may be adopted quickly, such as the consumption of fast food. Change is individualized and depends on the community, availability of native foods, family income, and the length of time the family has lived in the United States.[3]

Mexican Foods

Staple foods of Mexican-American families (especially those with limited incomes) include beans, rice, and tortillas. Homemade corn or flour tortillas are small, and 5 to 10 may be eaten at a meal. Flour tortillas purchased at a store are usually much larger, and one to two may be eaten. Tortillas are eaten in the home; bread is usually consumed away from home. Pinto beans, black beans, garbanzo beans, and kidney beans are popular and may be served several times every day: boiled for breakfast, fried for lunch, and refried for the evening meal. Rice may be prepared in soup with vegetables or meat or served with vegetables in which all the water has been steamed out. Rice also may be fried in oil before the water is added.

Protein foods include eggs, cheese, beef, pork, chicken, turkey, shrimp, red snapper, and other firm-fleshed fish. Many stuffed Mexican foods (eg, tacos, enchiladas, tamales, quesadillas, and burritos) have become staples in the American diet as well. Tamales are one of the oldest Mexican foods. The dough is usually made of masa harina (corn that has been dried, treated with lime, and finely ground into flour); this is sweetened or filled with meat or vegetables, folded into a corn husk, and steamed.[3]

Vegetables are usually a component of a dish, not served separately. Some common choices include cactus, carrots, chiles, corn, cucumber, jicama, onions, peas, potatoes, radishes, squash (chayote, pumpkin, summer), squash blossoms, tomatillos, tomatoes, and yucca. Hearty soups or stews are popular choices for lunch and dinner.

Common semitropical and tropical fruits include avocados, bananas, cactus fruit, cherimoya, coconut, guava, lemons, limes, mangos, melon, oranges, papaya, passion fruit, pineapple, plantains, strawberries, and zapote (fruit of the sapodilla tree). Many fruits are eaten in the form of *aguas* (water with pureed fruits and sugar added).

The most common traditional desserts are *arroz con leche* (rice pudding), *capirotada* (bread pudding), *buñuelos* or *sopapillas* (fritters), flan, and *pan dulce* (white bread with sugar, often made with lard; can also refer to pastry or cake).[3]

Coffee may be prepared with large amounts of sugar and whole milk. *Atole* is a warm, milk-based beverage flavored with chocolate, fruit, or nuts, and thickened with very finely ground masa (corn flour). Although natural fruit drinks are popular in Mexico, carbonated beverages are quickly incorporated into the diet once individuals are in the United States.[4] Few dairy products are consumed, with the exception of yogurt and yogurt drinks. Because tap water is unsafe in much of Mexico and Central America, new immigrants may need to be reassured that tap water is safe in the United States.

Food is often spicy (there are more than 90 varieties of chiles), but spicy sauces vary with the region of Mexico. Seasonings such as anise, cilantro, cinnamon, cocoa, cumin, epazote (a pungent herb, also called Mexican tea), garlic, mace, and vanilla are commonly used.[3] Chicken bouillon cubes are used to season rice, *fideos* (pasta), and sauces.

Puerto Rican Foods

Staple foods of Puerto Rico include rice and beans (often fried, sometimes topped with added oil). The most popular types of legumes are kidney beans and *gandules* (pigeon peas). Garbanzos (chickpeas), navy beans, and black-eyed peas are also common. *Viandas,* a group of starchy tubers, are frequently used before they ripen. Common *viandas* include the following:

- *arracacha* (resembles a white carrot and tastes like a mixture of carrot, celery, and cabbage)
- banana (unripe; a ripe banana is considered a fruit, not a *vianda*)
- breadfruit
- cassava (manioc, yuca)
- plantain (ripe)
- potato
- sweet potato (yellow, white)
- *tanier* (white, yellow)
- taro (dasheen, malanga)
- yam (orange, white)

For more information about *viandas* and other traditional Latino cuisine, see Raichlen's *Healthy Latin Cooking* or consult one of the many helpful online resources.[4]

Popular fruits and vegetables include avocados, bananas, beans, cashew apples (the fruit surrounding the cashew nut), coconuts, guavas, mangos, papayas, passion fruit, pineapple, *guanabaná* (soursop), several types of squash, and tomatoes.

Fish is more plentiful than meat. One of the most popular kinds of fish is *bacalao* (codfish), which is cured with salt and can be eaten fresh or dry; anyone following a sodium-controlled diet should not regularly eat *bacalao*. Other common fish include bonito, grouper, mackerel, salmon, red snapper, and tuna.

Sazón is a popular commercial spice blend, which is high in monosodium glutamate (MSG).

Sofrito is a seasoning sauce made by sautéing diced peppers, onions, garlic, cilantro, annatto seeds, and spices with pieces of fried pork or pork sausage. It also may contain tomatoes (more popular in cuisine of neighboring Cuba). *Sofrito* is a traditional base for many different dishes in Latin cuisine. It is almost always used in rice dishes and is typically served in main meals. It is high in sodium and always contains some type of fat. It can be purchased already prepared.

Café con leche, strong coffee with hot milk and sugar, is a popular beverage. It is not a foamy drink and is usually three-quarters coffee. When prepared for children, more milk is usually added.

Tembleque is the Puerto Rican version of flan.

Nutrition Care

Cuban Foods

Cuban food practices are similar to those of the Puerto Rican community. Staple foods of Cuban-American families include rice, beans (especially black beans), and *viandas*. Black beans cooked with rice produce a dish called *congri*. *Tostones* are slices of fried unripe plantain. *Picadillo*, a beef hash flavored with *alcaparrado* (pickled olives, raisins, and capers), is a popular dish.[3]

Cubans eat many sweets made from fruits and *viandas*. A very popular and well-liked candy made from coconut is *panelitas*.

Central American Foods

El Salvador represents the traditions of Central America, whose customs are often similar to those of Mexico. El Salvador has an extensive coastline, so fish are plentiful. Tamales are usually encased in banana leaves rather than corn husks.[5]

Pupusa is a thick tortilla stuffed with cheese, beans, pork, or other foods, and it is one of the best-known Salvadorian foods. *Panes relleños* is a warm sandwich, much like a sub sandwich. Entrées include *paro salvadoreño*, or roast turkey with sauce, and *chicharrón*, which is cooked pork meat ground to a paste.

Casamiento, which translates as "marriage," is a dish of black beans and rice, just as in Cuban cuisine, although red beans are most popular in El Salvador. *Alguashte* (ground pumpkin seeds) are often used to thicken stews.

Quesadilla in Central America is a pound cake flavored with parmesan-like cheese and sour cream. A *pastelito* is a baked turnover. *Tres leches* cake is a very sweet cake drenched in three milks—sweetened condensed milk, evaporated milk, and heavy cream or half and half. *Semita* is a cake filled with jam, usually pineapple or guava jam.

Central American beverages include *horchata,* a sweet rice beverage, and *chichi,* a mildly alcoholic-fermented corn beverage.

Cheeses are named for their characteristics: *queso fresco*, soft cheese; *quesillo,* mild cheese; and *queso duro*, hard cheese.

The *viandas* specific to Central America are:

- *chiplin* (leafy green);
- *nance* (cherry-like fruit);
- *loroco* (vine flower bud native to Central America);
- *pacalla* (palm flower), which is usually breaded in cornmeal, fried, and served with tomato sauce; and
- *curtido*, a lightly fermented, spicy cabbage relish often served with *pupusas*.

South American Foods

Although most South Americans differentiate themselves from people of Mexican, Caribbean, or Central

American background, their food is somewhat similar in that it is largely corn-based, spiced with chili peppers, and commonly contains tomatoes. This book does not address South American foods specifically, but many of the food names are similar to those of other Latino cuisines.

References

1. Curry K, Jaffe A. *Nutrition Counseling and Communication Skills*. Philadelphia, PA: WB Saunders; 1998.

2. National Alliance for Hispanic Health. *A Primer for Cultural Proficiency: Towards Quality Health Services for Hispanics*. Washington, DC: Estrella Press; 2001. www.hrsa.gov/sites/default/files/culturalcompetence/servicesforhispanics.pdf. Accessed October 10, 2017.

3. Kittler PG, Sucher KP, Nahikian-Nelms M. *Food and Culture*. 7th ed. Boston, MA: Cengage Learning; 2017.

4. Raichlen S. *Steven Raichlen's Healthy Latin Cooking: 200 Sizzling Recipes from Mexico, Cuba, the Caribbean, Brazil, and Beyond*. New York, NY: Rodale Press; 1998.Easy Recipe for Making Tamales Salvadorenos—Chicken Tamales. Postres de la Cipota. www.postresdelacipota.com/2011/12/tamales-salvadorenos-feliz-ano-nuevo.html. Accessed December 28, 2017.

CHAPTER 4

Establishing a Counseling Relationship

Creating a Positive Nutrition Counseling Relationship

Some cultural values common to the Latino culture are *personalismo* (a preference for personal contact), *respeto* (respect), *confianza* (trust), and *las familias* (importance of family). Understanding these values is key to building a good professional relationship with Latino clients.[1]

Personal Contact

Oftentimes, Latino clients want a personal but not informal relationship with their health care providers. To personalize your approach and begin to build trust with the client, start by establishing a friendly atmosphere. Allow the client to get settled. Offer a glass of water. Ask questions about family roots, traditions, and recipes, if appropriate, before asking more formal questions.[1,2]

Respect

Show proper respect to your clients by greeting them formally by title and family name. If you are uncertain about how to pronounce a name, be sure to ask. Refrain from using a client's first name at the beginning of a relationship, unless the client is a child. If you are speaking Spanish, use the formal *usted* rather than the informal *tú* for "you," and be sure to greet the elder adults first.[1,2]

Shake hands at the beginning of each meeting. A firm and slightly extended handshake is appropriate. Latinos may show respect by avoiding eye contact with you, but they will expect you to look directly at them. This remains true even when you are working through an interpreter.[2] Also, they may wait to sit down until invited to do so.

Latino clients respect health care providers because of their knowledge of health, education, and training. However, they also expect to receive respect.[1,2] This is so important that your client may terminate the counseling relationship if he or she does not feel respected. For many Latinos, showing respect means not asking uncomfortable questions or expressing negative feelings, so you must gently encourage questions.[3]

Trust

Take the time needed to establish trust. If trust is not established, a client may avoid conflict or confrontation by signaling understanding or quickly agreeing to a treatment plan.[3] Once you have established a trusting relationship, your client may follow a treatment plan as a personal favor to you. [2,4]

One recommendation for building trust is letting clients know they should tell you if they prefer not to answer any of your questions.[5] Another is telling your client what you are writing in your notes.[1]

Family Involvement

For many Latinos, family can include friends, neighbors, and members of faith-based organizations, clubs, or teams. The family's needs may be placed ahead of those of the client, which can make changes in eating habits difficult. Involve the family, especially those involved with food preparation, in the nutrition counseling session.[1,3] For example, be prepared to offer alternate meal preparation methods for traditional foods.[1]

Be careful to note that because of regulatory issues and privacy concerns, you should respectfully obtain the client's consent for the family members to be present and possibly be privy to confidential issues.

Working With Interpreters

Interpreters (those who convert verbal language) and translators (those who work with written language) can help you provide effective nutrition counseling.

If you do not speak Spanish or if your client has no English language ability, using a trained interpreter who has expertise in the client's language and culture is best for both you and your client. In deference to the Latino culture, the ideal interpreter would be older than your client and of the same gender.[5]

If family members or friends are used as interpreters, your client may be reluctant to share certain concerns, and it may be more difficult for you to assess the client's understanding. Although children commonly are asked to interpret for parents, this practice should be a last resort because it places the parent and child in positions of reversed power and authority. In general, it is best to have Spanish-speaking staff or volunteers interpret if a professional interpreter is not available.[6] However, if staff are not familiar with medical terminology, they may unknowingly make mistakes.

Following are basic guidelines for working with interpreters. Most of these guidelines are also appropriate for working with clients with limited literacy skills.[2,3,5]

- Determine what questions you will ask before the counseling session begins. As much as possible, pare the questions down to the "need to know" variety.
- Be respectful of the client's questions.

- Use open-ended questions, such as "Tell me how you...," rather than questions that can be answered with yes or no.

- Learn a few words in your client's language (at least introductory greetings and good-byes).

- Speak in short sentences and ask one question at a time. Interpreters will have difficulty converting long statements without omitting something important. Your client also may have difficulty following long sentences.

- Avoid technical terminology, professional jargon, abstractions, and idioms and other expressions that would be unfamiliar to a nonnative English speaker.

- Make sure the client participates in the conversation, and look at and speak directly to the client, not the interpreter.[5,6]

- Even though you do not understand the language, listen and look for nonverbal cues when your client speaks to the interpreter.

- Schedule sufficient time. A session with an interpreter will take at least twice as long as usual.

- Have the interpreter ask the client to repeat the information communicated to see whether it is understood. (This also allows the client to ask questions.) Request that the interpreter use your client's exact words so that you can assess understanding more accurately.[5]

Nutrition Care

Cross-Cultural Communication

Communication and your relationship with your client are key to successful nutrition counseling. Success in counseling is measured not only by the provision of technically accurate information but also by the way in which the counseling is conducted.[5]

Client-centered counseling emphasizes the client's responsibility and active participation in designing a personal nutrition program. Some Latino clients may not respond well to this approach.[4] Because the Latino culture often places the family's needs before the needs of the individual, independence may not be valued. In addition, if clients feel powerless, they are less likely to believe that they can assume direct responsibility for their health.[5]

Listen to your client's personal cultural beliefs rather than assuming that he or she reflects the stereotypical Latino culture. Also, understand that your client's values and motivation are not necessarily the same as yours.[4] For example, because of cultural values, Latino mothers may be pleased when their infants or children are overweight. Thus, they do not react as expected when the nutrition professional offers calorie-lowering suggestions. It may be helpful to give an example of something that has worked for another client, but confirm that your client is interested in hearing the example.

To help clients feel comfortable sharing their feelings, try to convey acceptance by using phrases like

"I feel that . . ." Speak slowly, clearly, and in a conversational tone. Realize that raising the volume of your voice will not help your client understand—in fact, it is likely to be offensive.[4]

Nonverbal Communication

Nonverbal communication is important in counseling all clients. As previously noted, some Latino clients may be reluctant to make their real attitudes known directly; in such cases, nonverbal communication is even more important for counseling success.

Physical touch is the most personal form of nonverbal communication and thus its acceptability is highly variable among clients. Generally, a touch on the arm or brief pat on the shoulder is acceptable to clients with whom you are familiar.[2,5]

Individuals tend to believe what they see more than what they hear, so body language is important when you do not share a client's language. Try to convey warmth and acceptance with your body language.[7]

Closed Gestures

If you hold your arms or books in front of your torso or your hand in front of your face, you are displaying a "closed gesture," hiding yourself from those facing you.[7] This should be avoided.

Nutrition Care

Pointing

Pointing is acceptable if you need to identify a diagram or words on a paper. However, when you gesture toward your client, use your whole hand, not a single finger.[7]

Seating

Because your shoulders signal where your interest is, lean slightly forward with your upper body facing toward your client when you are seated. When the client is speaking, move closer and listen carefully. During conversation, Latinos may position themselves closer than you are accustomed to. If possible, have more than one chair available, and let your client choose a seat.[5,7] Some counselors and clients feel more comfortable angled toward each other instead of facing each other.[7]

Facial Expressions

Avoid frowning because it may make your client feel that you are skeptical about what is being said. This seems obvious, but many people frown while thinking about how to answer questions. If you wear eyeglasses, do not look over the rims or through the bottoms of your bifocals. Although a few nods are affirming, excessive nodding can be perceived negatively.[7]

Nutrition Care

Assessment of Health Beliefs and Practices

Medical anthropologist and noted cross-cultural expert Arthur Kleinman developed an interview tool that helps health care professionals obtain information in a culturally unbiased manner. The questions are open-ended and will increase your clients' comfort level, allowing them to be more open to your counseling suggestions. Following are a few of Kleinman's questions. Use your professional judgment to decide which of the questions to ask.[5]

- How can I help you today?
- What do you think caused this problem?
- What do you call this [problem] you are having? (Use the client's word[s] in place of "problem" and "it" in your follow-up questions.)
- Why do you think it started?
- What are the most important results you hope to receive from treatment?
- Would you like me to talk to anyone else in your family?
- Have you seen a healer for this problem? Are you using the suggested treatment?

Culturally Sensitive Interviewing

Once you have gained some understanding of your client's beliefs, continue with the interview. In 1983 Berlin and Fowkes developed the LEARN tool, a client-centered approach to culturally sensitive interviewing. Others have modified and enhanced the original tool.[5] The LEARN tool can help you negotiate a culturally sensitive nutrition treatment plan.

Listen Use active listening to demonstrate that what your client has to say is very important to you. This can help build your relationship.

Explain To make sure you understand accurately, restate (explain) what you think your client said. This lets your client correct misunderstandings or explain further.

Acknowledge Point out the similarities between what your client believes and what you feel is appropriate in the cause or treatment of the problem, then talk about the differences.

Recommend Give your client options that are culturally appropriate and practical. Provide the fewest options that still constitute proper nutrition care.

Negotiate As with any client, after discussing the options, ask where the client would like to begin.

References

1.   Klinger S, Brogan K. *Hispanic Family Nutrition: Complete Counseling Kit.* Chicago, IL: Academy of Nutrition and Dietetics; 2016.

2.   Salimbene S. Culture-sensitive health care: Hispanic. In: *What Language Does Your Patient Hurt In? A Practical Guide to Culturally Competent Care.* Amherst, MA: Diversity Resources; 2000.

3.   National Alliance for Hispanic Health. *A Primer for Cultural Proficiency: Towards Quality Health Services for Hispanics.* Washington, DC: Estrella Press; 2001. www.hrsa.gov/sites/default/files/culturalcompetence/servicesforhispanics.pdf. Accessed October 10, 2017.

4.   Curry K, Jaffe A. *Nutrition Counseling and Communication Skills.* Philadelphia, PA: WB Saunders; 1998.

5.   Boyle M. *Community Nutrition in Action.* 7th ed. Boston, MA: Cengage Learning; 2017.

6.   Kittler PG, Sucher KP, Nahikian-Nelms M. *Food and Culture.* 7th ed. Boston, MA: Cengage Learning; 2017.

7.   Desmond P, Copeland L. *Communicating with Today's Patient.* San Francisco, CA: Josey-Bass; 2000.

Nutrition Care

CHAPTER 5

Latino Health Profile

Notable Nutrition-Related Diseases in Latinos

The leading causes of death in Latinos are heart disease and cancer. Although cholesterol levels are similar to those in the non-Latino population, 41% of Latinos are unaware that they have high cholesterol levels; of those who are aware, only 29% receive treatment. Latinos are as likely as non-Latinos to have hypertension, but they are 24% more likely to have poorly controlled blood pressure and more likely to have a stroke than non-Latinos.[1-3]

The Latino population is disproportionately affected by diabetes and has a high prevalence of undetected diabetes, but there is considerable diversity as a function of Hispanic background.[4-6] However, Latinos have a 50% higher death rate for diabetes than non-Latinos.[1]

Obesity is more common in Latinos (especially Mexican-American women) than in the general population, with 42.5% of adults classified as obese, a significant increase since 1999.[4,5] Latinos also have very high rates of metabolic disease.[7]

Nutrition Concerns in Latino Children

Bottle-feeding is common among Latino groups, but where breastfeeding is practiced, there is a tendency to stop earlier and to introduce solid food earlier than current pediatric guidelines recommend.[7,8] Toddlers tend to feed from bottles (containing milk and sweetened drinks) longer than is recommended. Obesity among youths (ages 2 to 19) is highest in Latino children at 21.9%.[9]

Disease Prevention

Disease prevention is not highly valued in some Latino cultures, and thus Latinos have a higher prevalence of chronic illnesses than non-Latinos. Barriers to preventive care include lack of health insurance, limited health literacy, a shortage of Hispanic health care providers, and, in some cases, less access to healthful food choices. However, health promotion and disease prevention concepts seem to be gaining acceptance.[5]

References

1. Centers for Disease Control and Prevention. Vital signs: Hispanic health. May 2015. www.cdc.gov/vitalsigns /pdf/2015-05-vitalsigns.pdf. Accessed March 5, 2017.

2. Rodriguez CJ, Cai J, Swett K, et al. High cholesterol awareness, treatment, and control among Hispanics/Latinos: results from the Hispanic community health study/study of Latinos. *J Am Heart Assoc.* 2015;4:e001867.

3. American Heart Association. High cholesterol in Hispanics infographic. http://news.heart.org/nearly-half-of-hispanics-with-high-cholesterol-dont-realize-it/high -cholesterol-in-hispanics-3. Accessed June 6, 2017.

4. Trust for America's Health and Robert Wood Johnson Foundation. Special report: racial and ethnic disparities in obesity. 2014. http://stateofobesity.org/disparities/latinos. Accessed June 20, 2017.

5. Velasco-Mondragon E, Jimenez A, Palladino-Davis AG, Davis D, Escamilla-Cejudo JA. Hispanic health in the USA: a scoping review of the literature. *Public Health Reviews.* 2016;37(31):1-27.

6. Schneiderman N, Llabre M, Cowie CC, et al. Prevalence of diabetes among Hispanics/Latinos from diverse backgrounds: The Hispanic Community Health Study/Study of Latinos (HCHS/SOL). *Diabetes Care.* 2014;37:2233-2239.

7. Kittler PG, Sucher KP, Nahikian-Nelms M. *Food and Culture.* 7th ed. Boston, MA: Cengage Learning; 2017.

8.   Jones, KM, Power ML, Queenan JT, Schulkin J. Racial
      and ethnic disparities in breastfeeding. *Breastfeed Med.*
      2015;10(4):186-196.

9.   Nyberg K, Ramirez A, Gallion K. *Addressing Nutrition,
      Overweight and Obesity Among Latino Youth.* Robert Wood
      Johnson Foundation. December 2011. www.rwjf.org/content
      /dam/farm/reports/issue_briefs/2011/rwjf71859. Accessed
      June 20, 2017.

CHAPTER 6

Effective Communication

Communicating Nutrition Information to Latino Clients

The following specific guidelines will help you to communicate nutrition information to your Latino clients.

Language Skills

Some clients may not read or write Spanish or English. If a trained interpreter is not available, they may need to bring a family member (who may or may not read either language) to the counseling session. (Reminder: Because of regulatory issues and privacy concerns, obtain your client's consent before allowing family members to be present and privy to possibly confidential issues.)

Indirect Approach

When seeking information, an indirect approach may lower the risk of misunderstanding and hurt feelings. Make observations rather than judgments about behaviors.[1,2] For example, try to say "some people" rather than "you" when making comments. Use open-ended questions (eg, "How do you cook vegetables?") rather than a question that can be answered with a simple yes or no (eg, "Do you cook vegetables without salt?").[3]

Key Messages

Most people, including clients, do not speak the standard language of nutrition professionals. Therefore, focus on key messages and essential skills and behaviors rather than on information that may simply be nice to have.[4]

In her book, *15-Minute Consultation*, Lorena Drago cautions against the use of nutrition jargon. This jargon includes concept, category, and value words. Concept words require clinical knowledge (such as a healthy or balanced diet); category words describe foods that share similar characteristics (such as carbohydrates); and value/judgment words are quantitative but also subjective (such as moderation).[5]

Positive Food Practices

Even when a client simply needs guidance in selecting healthful foods, it is important to understand the individual's level of acculturation. Encourage clients to maintain the healthful foods in their traditional diet, such as fruits, vegetables, beans, and whole grains. Be ready to offer help in modifying traditional foods or in learning to use available foods. Examples include using a slow-cooker to prepare beans; preparing foods in advance and freezing; and educating about fruits and vegetables that may not be familiar but might be more affordable.[6]

Folk Beliefs

If a belief—such as placing a safety pin over a pregnant woman's abdomen to protect against the "evil eye"—causes no harm, do not offer an opinion of the practice. (See Chapter 2.)

Teaching and Learning Implications

Conveying nutrition information to clients with limited literacy or limited English language skills can be frustrating for both the nutrition professional and the client. Limited literacy does not mean limited intelligence or motivation. Any client who is ill, afraid, or under stress may have trouble understanding your counseling suggestions.[7] Thus, exclusive use of oral teaching is not an effective technique.[4]

When oral teaching is supplemented with easy-to-read materials (such as materials using words that are familiar and meaningful to clients), clients understand and retain information better. Additionally, Latino clients often have family members who can assist in the use and understanding of such materials.[8,9] Nutrition professionals must learn to develop or select easy-to-read educational materials for all clients. It is also important to have materials (in appropriate reading level in Spanish) that you are comfortable using.

Personalization also aids understanding and is important to most clients. If possible, personalize printed materials by rewriting key points, by circling the applicable points, or by crossing out text that does not apply to a particular client. Write in large, easy-to-read print.[4] (See Section III for more information on health literacy and easy-to-read education materials.) Actual food packages, food models, and measuring cups and spoons may help clients with limited English-language skills.[5]

Behavior Change Models

For nutrition counseling to succeed, the counselor must understand what motivates the client to change behavior. Many theories (or models) have been proposed to explain how people make decisions to change their behaviors. One, the locus of control theory, applies to many Latinos. For comparison, the stages of change (transtheoretical) model and the health belief model are summarized as well.

Locus of Control

The health locus of control theory (based on social cognitive theory) addresses the degree to which individuals believe that their health is controlled by themselves or by "powerful others." A client with an *internal* locus of control believes that health outcomes are directly the result of his or her behavior. In contrast, Latino clients often have an *external* locus of control, believing that fate, luck, or chance is in control.

Clients with an external locus of control are likely to hold the nutrition professional directly responsible for determining the appropriate action plan.[4] In their book, *Nutrition Counseling and Communication Skills,* Katharine Curry, PhD, RD, and Amy Jaffe, MS, RD, LD, provide an example of promoting behavior change without challenging the beliefs of a client with an external locus of control[8]:

CLIENT: *"My high blood sugar won't go away. I guess it is just my fate."*

DIETITIAN: *"Yes, I see. I have worked with some people with high blood sugar and it has been possible to control blood sugar fairly well. There is a nutrition plan that could have some effect on your blood sugar. Would you like to try it?"*

The importance of the family can also be used to motivate behavior change in Latino clients.[6] Adults unwilling to make changes to benefit their own health may be motivated to change for the sake of their children.

Stages of Change (Transtheoretical Model)

The stages of change model was developed by Prochaska and DiClemente in 1986 to understand smoking cessation behaviors.[4] In this model, behavior change is explained as readiness to change. The stages are as follows:

- **Precontemplation** The client is unaware or uninterested in making a change. Advice on nutrition changes is counterproductive at this stage.[10]
- **Contemplation** The client is thinking about making a change within the next 6 months.
- **Preparation** The client decides to make the change and plans to do so within the next month.
- **Action** The client is trying to make the change and has been working at it for less than 6 months.
- **Maintenance** The client works to sustain the change for 6 months or longer.

In nutrition counseling, difficulties arise when the intervention and the client's stage of change are mismatched.[8] Note that written materials and counseling styles are often geared toward action, even though most clients are in the precontemplation or contemplation stages.

Health Belief Model

The health belief model was developed by the US Public Health Service in the 1950s to explain why people (especially those at high risk) did not participate in programs designed to detect or prevent disease. The model theorizes that clients are unlikely to take a health action unless they believe:

- their health is in jeopardy;
- the disease would have serious effects, such as pain or loss of income;
- the benefits of taking action outweigh the costs of no action (and the action is within their grasp); or
- there is a compelling "cue" for them to take action.

Cues to action include advice from respected sources (possibly a nutrition professional), media campaigns, or a friend's illness.[4] Generally, a person's attitude toward the "nutrition lifestyle" is reflective of his or her attitude toward health.[8]

Assessing Learning: Teach-Back Method

The teach-back or show-me method—asking clients to repeat, in their own words, the essential information until they can summarize it correctly—is an effective strategy for confirming understanding. The teach-back method is not a test of the client's knowledge but a test of how well the professional has explained the concepts. It is helpful to remind the client that it is your responsibility to communicate the information clearly.

"We covered a lot today, and I want to make sure I explained things clearly. So let's review. What are the three things that will help you control your blood sugar?"

"What might you tell your family about what we have discussed?"

If clients cannot remember or accurately repeat the information, clarify or repeat it, then allow them to teach it back again. Repeat this until they can correctly communicate the information in their own words.[11]

References

1. Boyle M. *Community Nutrition in Action*. 7th ed. Boston, MA: Cengage Learning; 2017.

2. Kittler PG, Sucher KP, Nahikian-Nelms M. *Food and Culture*. 7th ed. Boston, MA: Cengage Learning; 2017.

3. Salimbene S. Culture-sensitive health care: Hispanic. In: *What Language Does Your Patient Hurt In? A Practical Guide to Culturally Competent Care*. Amherst, MA: Diversity Resources; 2000.

4. Redman BK. *The Process of Patient Education*. 7th ed. St. Louis, MO: Mosby Year Book; 1993.

5. Drago L. *15-Minute Consultation: Tips, Tools and Activities to Make Your Counseling More Effective*. Chicago, IL: Academy of Nutrition and Dietetics; 2017.

6.   Klinger SM. *Hispanic Family Nutrition: Complete Counseling Kit.* Chicago, IL: Academy of Nutrition and Dietetics; 2016.

7.   Root J, Stableford S. *Write it Easy-to-Read: A Guide to Creating Plain English Materials.* Biddeford, ME: University of New England; 1998.

8.   Curry K, Jaffe A. *Nutrition Counseling and Communication Skills.* Philadelphia, PA: WB Saunders; 1998.

9.   Juckett G. Caring for Latino patients. *Am Fam Physician.* 2013;87:48-54.

10. Mahan LK, Raymond JL. *Krause's Food and the Nutrition Care Process.* 14th ed. St. Louis, MO: Elsevier; 2017.

11. US Department of Health and Human Services Agency for Healthcare Research and Quality. *AHRQ Health Literacy Universal Precautions Toolkit.* 2nd ed. www.ahrq.gov /professionals/quality-patient-safety/quality-resources /tools/literacy-toolkit/index.html. Accessed June 25, 2017.

Section II

Spanish Grammar and Vocabulary for the Nutrition Professional

CHAPTER 7

Spanish Pronunciation and Adjectives

When using the pronunciation key for a word, place the stress on the syllable in all uppercase letters.

Vowels and Consonants

Spanish is a phonetic language and therefore is considered relatively easy to pronounce. Unlike English, the vowels in Spanish have a single sound regardless of where they appear in a word. Although most consonants have the same or similar sounds in English and Spanish, several consonants are pronounced differently in Spanish. The following points will help with your pronunciation.

E A cross between the English *a* in words like *cake* or *bake* and the English short *e*, as in *bed*.

Examples: *mesa, tres, Pepe, peso*

G
(followed by e or i)
Pronounced like the English *h*.

Examples: *gigante, gente, giro, inteligente, Gerardo*

H Always silent in Spanish pronunciation.

Examples: *hola, hermano, Hugo, honesto, hogar*

I Always pronounced like an English long *e* sound, as in *beef* or *creek*.

Examples: *gris, piso, triste, privado, liso*

J Always pronounced like the English *h*, as in *hunger* or *happy*.

Examples: *José, Julia, juro, tejer, burbuja*

LL In most of Latin America and the United States, this is pronounced like the English consonant *y*, as in *yak*. In some parts of South America, it can be pronounced like the English *j* in *joke* or *sh* in *shake*; those who pronounce *ll* this way will likely also pronounce the consonant *y* the same way.

Examples: *llama, llorar, Vallarta, llanto, amarillo*

Ñ Pronounced *ny* as in the English words *onion* or *bunion*.

Examples: *ñame, mañana, español, año, compañía*

The tilde (the curving line that appears above the n) differentiates the pronunciation of n and ñ. Some words in Spanish differ only in the pronunciation of this single letter but mean two different things, such as campana *(bell) and* campaña *(campaign).*

R/RR When a word begins with *r*, it is always trilled. (English does not have this sound. Think of it as a slightly prolonged *r* sound.) *RR* is considered one letter in the Spanish alphabet and is also trilled, no matter where it appears in the word.

Examples: *rosa, rojo, perro, ferrocarril*

R Always "tapped" when it is within or at the end of a word. This is similar to the *tt* sound in American English (as opposed to British English) in words like *butter, better, pitter,* or *patter.*

Examples: *para, pero, hablar, caro, sudadera*

V In most of Latin America and the United States, pronunciation is a combination of the English *v* and *b*. (For the nonnative speaker of Spanish, it will probably sound closer to the English *b*.) In some parts of Spain, *v* is pronounced as it is in English, as in *victory*.
Examples: *Valencia, Victor, veinte, vaca, vacaciones*

Z In most of Latin America and the United States, pronounced like the English *s*, as in *Sara, syrup*, or *tacos*. In Spain, this consonant is pronounced like the English *th* in *thistle*.
Examples: *Pizarra, zapato, Zócalo, zurdo, zorro*

Other differences in the pronunciation of consonants depend on geographical region. For example, in parts of Puerto Rico and the Caribbean, *r* may be pronounced like *l* and vice versa. (This is similar to the Chinese pronunciation of these consonants.) However, most standard Spanish will be pronounced as outlined above.

Spanish speakers, like English speakers, tend to blend syllables together, which gives the impression that Spanish is spoken rapidly. This will be frustrating at first, but by listening to native speakers of Spanish, you should eventually become accustomed to it. Try listening to a Spanish radio station or watching a Spanish television channel, such as Telemundo or Univisión, to get used to hearing Spanish.

Adjectives

Gendered Adjectives

In Spanish, nouns are either masculine or feminine in gender. Adjectives that describe a noun must match the gender. Usually, but not always, masculine nouns will end in *o*, and feminine nouns will end in *a*. However, there are nouns that end in other vowels or in consonants. Therefore, it will not always be clear which form of the adjective should be used. When in doubt as to the gender of the noun, you may need to guess the adjectival form.

Many adjectives ending in the letter *o* can be changed to end with the letter *a*. In this book, variations of these adjectives are noted with the ending *o/a* (for example, *descremado/a* [skim]). Which ending to use will depend on the gender of the noun that the adjective is describing.

For example, *queso* (cheese) is a masculine noun. Therefore, if you refer to skim cheese, you would use the masculine adjective *descremado* (ending in *o*). On the other hand, when speaking about skim milk, you would use the feminine version of the adjective, *descremada*, because *leche* (milk) is a feminine noun.

Plural Adjectives

If a noun is plural, the adjective must also be made plural by adding an *s* to the end. For example, *fresh apple* is *manzana fresca,* whereas the plural is *manzanas frescas.* (Note that the Spanish word for *apples* is feminine, so the singular form of the adjective ends in *a*.)

Placement of Adjectives

In Spanish, adjectives are generally placed after nouns. This is different than English, in which adjectives are placed before nouns. For example, *skim cheese* (adjective, noun) in Spanish is *queso descremado* (noun, adjective).

You may want to refer to a Spanish grammar text, where these concepts will be explained in detail. Even if you are uncertain about the rules, don't be shy about trying to speak Spanish with your clients. In all but the rarest of cases, they will be happy that you are able to communicate in their language and will forgive your incorrect grammar.

CHAPTER 8

Introductory Conversation

This chapter presents some of the words and phrases you will need in an introductory conversation with a Spanish-speaking person.

Greetings

English	Español	Pronunciation
Hello/Hi	*Hola*	OH-lah
Good morning	*Buenos días*	BWEH-nohs DEE-yahs
	Buen día	bwehn DEE-yah[a]
Good afternoon	*Buenas tardes*	BWEH-nahs TAHR-dehs
Good evening	*Buenas noches*	BWEH-nahs NOH-chehs

[a] Buen dia *is often pronounced as if it is one word, bwehn-DEE-yah.*

Most Spanish-speaking people will shake hands and respond:

Español	Pronunciation	English
Mucho gusto	MOO-choh GOO-stoh	Pleased to meet you
Encantada [only used by females, to people of both genders]	ehn-kahn-TAH-thah	Pleased to meet you
Encantado [only used by males, to people of both genders]	ehn-kahn-TAH-thoh	Pleased to meet you
Hola, buenos días/ tardes/noches	OH-lah, BWEH-nohs DEE-yahs/ TAHR-dehs/ NOH-chehs	Hello, good morning/afternoon/ evening

Spanish Basics

Cultural Tidbit

It is customary in Hispanic culture for two women, or a man and a woman, to greet each other with a kiss on one or both cheeks. This gesture is usually reserved for friends, but it is possible that someone you have just met may attempt to kiss your cheek, or possibly hug you. If a client greets you in this way, it may be considered rude if you do not reciprocate.

How Are You?

English	Español	Pronunciation
How are you?	¿Cómo está usted?	KOH-moh eh-STAH oo-STEHD?
(Very) fine/well	(Muy) bien	(moo-wee) bee-EHN
So-so	Así, así Más o menos	ah-SEE, ah-SEE mahs oh MEH-nohs
Not very well	No muy bien	noh moo-wee bee-EHN
(Very) bad	(Muy) mal	(moo-wee) mahl

After responding, most people will say:

Español	Pronunciation	English
Gracias, ¿y usted?	GRAH-see-ahs, ee oo-STEHD?	Thank you, and you?

What Is Your Name?

English	Español	Pronunciation
What is your name?	¿Cómo se llama usted?	KOH-moh seh YAH-mah oo-STEHD?
	¿Cuál es su nombre?	kwahl ehs soo NOHM-breh?
My name is …	Me llamo …	meh YAH-moh …
	Mi nombre es …	mee NOHM-breh ehs …

What Country Are You From?

English	Español	Pronunciation
What country are you from?	¿De qué país es usted?	deh keh pah-EES ehs oo-STEHD?[a]
I am from...	(Yo) soy de...	(yoh) soy deh...

[a] Es usted *is often pronounced as if it is one word, eh-soo-STEHD.*

Titles in Spanish

English	Español	Pronunciation
Mrs.	Señora	sehn-YOH-rah
Miss/Ms.	Señorita	sehn-yoh-REE-tah
Mr.	Señor	sehn-YOHR

It is a common sign of respect to use these titles, even without including surnames, when greeting someone. For example, *Hola, Señora,* or *Hola, Señor. ¿Cómo está usted?* If a woman is pregnant, use *señora*, regardless of whether or not she is married.

The titles *Don* (Dohn) and *Doña* (DOHN-yah) are used before first names with older friends, neighbors, or godparents. You probably will not want to use these titles with clients, at least until you are better acquainted with them.

Cultural Tidbit

Latinos tend to position themselves closer to others than non-Latino Americans may be comfortable with (we may feel they are encroaching on personal space). In general, Latinos may touch each other more than non-Latino Americans. Physical demonstrations of affection and care, such as a kiss on the cheek or a pat on the back when saying goodbye, are generally appreciated by Latinos.

Ways to Say Good-bye

English	Español	Pronunciation
Good-bye	*Adiós*	ah-dee-YOHS
	Chao/Chau	chow
See you later	*Hasta luego*	AH-stah loo-WEH-goh
	Hasta la vista	AH-stah lah VEE-stah
See you tomorrow	*Hasta mañana*	AH-stah mahn-YAH-nah
See you soon	*Hasta pronto*	AH-stah PROHN-toh
We'll see each other	*Nos vemos*	nohs BEH-mohs
See you next time	*Hasta la próxima*	AH-stah lah PROHK-see-mah

You should practice these introductory words and phrases until they become second nature. Any Spanish-speaking person you encounter will probably be happy to exchange pleasantries with you. But beware: If you begin speaking Spanish with a native speaker, he or she might want to continue the conversation, speaking rapidly and saying things you don't understand. What do you say? Here are two options:

Español	Pronunciation	English
Lo siento, pero hablo muy poco español.	loh see-YEHN-toh, PEH-roh AH-bloh moo-wee POH-koh eh-spahn-YOHL	I'm sorry, but I speak very little Spanish.
¿Podría hablar más despacio, por favor?	poh-DREE-ah ah-BLAHR mahs des-PAH-see-oh, pohr fah-BOHR?	Could you please speak more slowly?

CHAPTER 9

Numbers from 1 to 3,000

From 0 to 15

Numbers in Spanish follow a series of patterns, just as they do in English. The first group of numbers must be memorized.

Number	Español	Pronunciation
zero	*Cero*	SEH-roh
one	*Uno*	OO-noh
two	*Dos*	dohs
three	*Tres*	trehs
four	*cuatro*	KWAH-troh
five	*cinco*	SEEN-koh

Number	Español	Pronunciation
six	*seis*	SEH-ees
seven	*siete*	see-EH-teh
eight	*ocho*	OH-choh
nine	*nueve*	noo-EH-beh
ten	*diez*	dee-ehs
eleven	*once*	OHN-seh
twelve	*doce*	DOH-seh
thirteen	*trece*	TREH-seh
fourteen	*catorce*	kah-TOHR-seh
fifteen	*quince*	KEEN-seh

Spanish Basics

From 16 to 99

Beginning with 16, Spanish numbers follow a pattern whereby the number starts with the number of tens, followed by *y* (the word for *and*; pronounced ee), then the number of ones. For example, 16 (ten and six) is *diez y seis* (dee-ehs ee SEH-ees, though it is often pronounced as one word run together, dee-ehs-see-SEH-ees).

Notice that the Spanish word for 16 can also be written as *dieciséis*. The one-word spelling is much more common, but the three-word spelling is a bit easier to

remember. Just remember to pronounce the three words
as one.

Because all Spanish numbers from 16 to 99 follow
this same pattern, it is only necessary to memorize the
numbers for 20, 30, 40, 50, 60, 70, 80, and 90.

Number	Español	Pronunciation
twenty	*veinte*	BEHN-teh
thirty	*treinta*	TREHN-tah
forty	*cuarenta*	kwah-REHN-tah
fifty	*cincuenta*	seen-KWEHN-tah
sixty	*sesenta*	seh-SEHN-tah
seventy	*setenta*	seh-TEHN-tah
eighty	*ochenta*	oh-CHEHN-tah
ninety	*noventa*	noh-BEHN-tah

When you want to express a number within these
units of ten, simply add *y* and then the number from one
to nine. For example, 66 is *sesenta y seis* (seh-sehn-tah ee
SEH-ees). These numbers are usually pronounced rapidly like a single word instead of three separate words.

From 100 to 3,000

Number	Español	Pronunciation
one hundred[a]	*cien*	see-EHN
	ciento	see-EHN-toh
two hundred	*doscientos*	dohs-see-EHN-tohs
three hundred	*trescientos*	trehs-see-EHN-tohs
four hundred	*cuatrocientos*	kwah-troh-see-EHN-tohs
five hundred	*quinientos*	kee-nee-YEHN-tohs
six hundred	*seiscientos*	see-ehs-see-EHN-tohs
seven hundred	*setecientos*	seh-teh-see-EHN-tohs
eight hundred	*ochocientos*	oh-choh-see-EHN-tohs
nine hundred	*novecientos*	noh-beh-see-EHN-tohs
one thousand	*mil* (Tip: think "millennium")	meel
two thousand	*dos mil*	dohs meel
three thousand	*tres mil*	trehs meel

[a] Cien *is used when the number is exactly 100.* Ciento *is used when another number follows* cien—*for example,* ciento uno *(101).*

In numbers from 100 to 999, no *y* is needed between the hundred number and the number being added. For example: 356 is *trescientos cincuenta y seis* (trehs-see-EHN-tohs seen-KWEN-tah ee SEH-ees), **not** *trescientos y cincuenta y seis*. Likewise, the *y* is also not used when stating numbers in the thousands. For example: 25,589 is *veinticinco mil, quinientos ochenta y nueve* (behn-teh-seen-koh MEEL, kee-nee-YEHN-tohs oh-chen-tah ee noo-EH-beh).

Cultural Tidbit

When writing numbers, people in some Spanish-speaking countries use periods where commas would appear in the United States, and vice versa. For example, what is written as *25,589* in the United States might be *25.589* in Spanish-speaking countries. It is important to discover which system of punctuation a client uses to avoid miscommunication. Also, a written *1* may look like a *7*, and a written *7* might have a horizontal line drawn through the vertical line.

The best way to learn Spanish numbers is to practice counting. Try to get in the habit of counting in Spanish in the shower, at a stoplight, or when doing your sit-ups. Any time you would normally count in English, count in Spanish instead.

CHAPTER 10

Telling Time and Days of the Week

Discussing Time With Your Client

When interacting with clients, you typically will not be asking them what time it is, but rather at what time they did something. "At what time?" is expressed as *¿A qué hora?* (ah keh OH-rah?; *qué hora* is often pronounced as one word, keh-OH-rah). This question is answered using one of the following two formulas:

A la (ah lah) + the time of day for any time between 1:00 and 1:59.

A las (ah lahs) + time of day for any time between 2:00 and 12:59.

Follow these examples:

English	Español	Pronunciation
At what time?	*¿A qué hora?*	ah keh OH-rah?[a]
At 1:00	*A la una*	ah lah OO-nah
At 2:00	*A las dos*	ah lahs dohs
At 3:00	*A las tres*	ah lahs trehs

[a] Qué hora *is often pronounced as one word,* keh-OH-rah

When the time is not exactly on the hour, the minutes are simply added to the hour, using the conjunction *y* (and; pronounced ee) or the preposition *con* (with; pronounced kohn).

English	Español	Pronunciation
At 1:12	*A la una y doce*	ah lah OO-nah ee DOH-seh
	A la una con doce	ah lah OO-nah kohn DOH-seh
At 9:20	*A las nueve y veinte*	ah lahs noo-EH-beh ee BEHN-teh
	A las nueve con veinte	ah lahs noo-EH-beh kohn BEHN-teh

When the time is quarter past or half past the hour, the following phrases are often used:

English	Español	Pronunciation
quarter after	*y cuarto*	ee KWAHR-toh
half past	*y media*	ee MEH-thee-yah

For example:

English	Español	Pronunciation
At 5:15	*A las cinco y cuarto*	ah lahs SEEN-koh ee KWAHR-toh
At 10:30	*A las diez y media*	ah lahs dee-EHS ee MEH-thee-yah

Although *y cuarto* and *y media* are most often used to express these times, it is also acceptable to use the numbers *quince* (KEEN-seh) and *treinta* (TREHN-tah).

There are two ways to express the time when it is more than half (between 31 minutes and 59 minutes) past the hour. The simplest way is to simply add the minutes to the hour, as in the previous examples.

English	Español	Pronunciation
At 1:55	*A la una y cincuenta y cinco*	ah lah OO-nah ee seen-KWEHN-tah ee SEEN-koh
At 12:45	*A las doce y cuarenta y cinco*	ah lahs DOH-seh ee kwah-REHN-tah ee SEEN-koh

The second way is to choose the next hour, and then subtract the minutes left until that hour strikes, using the word *menos* (MEH-nohs) or *para* (PAH-rah). For example, 1:55 could be expressed in three ways:

A la una y cincuenta y cinco
(ah lah OO-nah ee seen-KWEHN-tah ee SEEN-koh)

A las dos menos cinco
(ah lahs dohs meh-nohs SEEN-koh)

Cinco para las dos
(SEEN-koh PAH-rah lahs dohs)

The latter two ways are more commonly used, but it may be easier for you to simply add the minutes to the hour.

AM or PM?

There are two ways to indicate morning, afternoon, or night, depending on whether a specific hour or general time is given.

Specific Hour

When using these phrases in conjunction with a specific hour:

English	Español	Pronunciation
in the morning	*de la mañana*	deh lah mahn-YAH-nah
in the afternoon	*de la tarde*	deh lah TAHR-deh
at night	*de la noche*	deh lah NOH-cheh

For example:

English	Español	Pronunciation
At 8:00 in the morning	*A las ocho de la mañana*	Ah lahs OH-choh deh lah mahn-YAH-nah
At 3:30 in the afternoon	*A las tres y media de la tarde*	ah lahs trehs ee MEH-dee-ah deh lah TAHR-deh

Number	Español	Pronunciation
At 7:45 at night	*A las ocho menos cuarto de la noche*	ah lahs OH-choh MEH-nohs KWAHR-toh deh lah NOH-cheh

General Time of Day

English	Español	Pronunciation
in the morning	*por la mañana*	pohr lah mahn-YAH-nah
	en la mañana	ehn lah mahn-YAH-nah
in the afternoon	*por la tarde*	pohr lah TAHR-deh
	en la tarde	ehn lah TAHR-deh
at night	*por la noche*	pohr lah NOH-cheh
	en la noche	ehn lah NOH-cheh

Military Time

Some Spanish speakers may be accustomed to using military time because it is the practice in some countries. In military time, the hours of the day are counted from 0 (midnight) to 23 (11:00 PM)—1:00 PM is 1300, 2:00 PM is 1400, and so on. For example, *at 1615* (4:15 PM) would be *a las dieciséis y cuarto* (ah lahs dee-ehs-ee-SEH-ees ee KWAHR-toh).

Days of the Week

English	Español	Pronunciation
Monday	*lunes*	LOOH-nehs
Tuesday	*martes*	MAHR-tehs
Wednesday	*miércoles*	mee-YEHR-koh-lehs
Thursday	*jueves*	HWEH-behs
Friday	*viernes*	bee-YEHR-nehs
Saturday	*sábado*	SAH-bah-thoh
Sunday	*domingo*	doh-MEEN-goh

CHAPTER 11

What Do You Eat?
When Do You Eat?

Eating Habits

Individuals in Spanish-speaking countries generally enjoy three meals each day and occasional snacks, much like individuals in the United States. Of course, the content of those meals will vary greatly, as will the size of the meals and the time of day they are eaten.

In the United States, dinner is generally considered the main meal of the day and is consumed in the early to mid-evening. In contrast, individuals in most Spanish-speaking countries consider lunch their main meal, and dinner is usually lighter and eaten in the evening. Many stores and businesses in these countries, particularly in Spain, close for a few hours at mid-day so that all family members can enjoy their main meal together, although this practice is not as prevalent as it once was, especially in large cities. Children generally come home from school to have lunch. Sometimes people take a *siesta* (see-EH-stah), a short afternoon nap, after lunch.

Breakfast in Spanish-speaking countries tends to be lighter than a traditional American breakfast. Breakfast consists of strong coffee, juices, fresh fruits, sweet breads, and pastries. Sometimes eggs and a breakfast meat may be served. Beans are a staple breakfast food in Mexico and Central America but not in the Caribbean. Breakfast is usually eaten at about the same time (early to mid-morning) as in the United States.

A snack is usually eaten between lunch and dinner, at around 5 or 6 PM. This may consist of sweet bread, pastries, *churros* (sweet, deep-fried dough; pronounced CHOO-rrohs), cookies, and hot drinks, such as coffee or hot chocolate.

These are general characteristics of Latino mealtimes and eating habits. Just as there are different Spanish-speaking countries and cultures, there is great variety in the foods that are consumed.

Names of Meals

English	Español	Pronunciation
breakfast	*desayuno*[a]	deh-sah-YOO-noh

[a] *Sometimes the term* desayuno *can be used to mean lunch as well.*

Number	Español	Pronunciation
lunch	*almuerzo*	ahl-MWEHR-soh
	comida	koh-MEE-thah
	lonche	LOHN-cheh
dinner	*cena*	SEH-nah
snack	*merienda*	meh-ree-EHN-dah
	bocadillo	boh-kah-DEE-yoh
	entrecomidas	ehn-treh-koh-MEE-thahs

Spanish Basics

Times of Meals

Desayuno (breakfast) is normally eaten:
   por la mañana
   (pohr lah mahn-YAH-nah)
   in the morning

Almuerzo, comida, or *lonche* (lunch) is generally eaten:
   por la tarde
   (pohr lah TAHR-deh)
   in the afternoon

Cena (dinner) is eaten:
   por la noche
   (pohr lah NOH-cheh)
   at night

Common Adverbs

English	Español	Pronunciation
always	*siempre*	see-EHM-preh
generally	*generalmente*	heh-neh-rahl-MEHN-teh
never	*nunca*	NOON-kah
normally	*normalmente*	nohr-mahl-MEHN-teh
usually	*usualmente*	oo-soo-ahl-MEHN-teh

Basic Questions and Answers

Some questions and phrases relating to meals are:

English	Español	Pronunciation
Do you eat . . . ?	*¿Come usted . . . ?*	KOH-me oo-STEHD?
When?	*¿Cúando?*	KWAHN-doh?
I eat . . .	*(Yo) como . . . a*	(yoh) KOH-moh
I don't eat . . .	*(Yo) no como . . . a*	(yoh) noh KOH-moh
Are you hungry?	*¿Tiene usted hambre?*	tee-EHN-neh oo-STEHD AHM-breh?
Are you thirsty?	*¿Tiene usted sed?*	tee-EHN-neh oo-STEHD sehd?
I am hungry.	*(Yo) tengo hambre.*[a]	(yoh) TEHN-goh AHM-breh

Number	Español	Pronunciation
I am thirsty.	*(Yo) tengo sed.*[a]	(yoh) TEHN-goh sehd
I am full.	*(Yo) estoy satisfecho/a.*[ab]	(yoh) ehs-TOY sah-tees-FEH-choh/ah[b].

[a] Yo (I) *is optional.*
[b] *These adjectives can end in either the letter "o" or "a," depending on the gender of the noun that the adjective modifies. See Chapter 7 for more on this topic.*

Practice Dialogues

These questions and answers can be combined with what you have already learned to form dialogues. Read the following dialogue between a nutrition professional and a client (presented in English on the left, in Spanish on the right).

In Spanish, *nutrition professional* is *nutricionista* (noo-tree-see-oh-NEES-tah) or *nutrióloga* (noo-tree-OH-loh-gah) and *client* is *cliente* (klee-YEHN-teh).

NUTRITION PROFESSIONAL:
Good morning, Mrs. Mendoza. It's good to meet you. I am Ms. Smith, your dietitian.

NUTRICIONISTA:
Buenos días, Señora Mendoza. Es un placer conocerla. Soy la Señora Smith, su nutricionista.
(BWEH-nohs THEE-ahs, seen-YOH-rah mehn-DOH-sah. ehs oon plah-SEHR koh-noh-SEHR-lah. soy lah seen-YOH-rah smeeth, soo noo-tree-see-oh-NEES-tah.)

CLIENT:
It is good to meet
you, too.

CLIENTE:
Mucho gusto.
(MOO-choh GOO-stoh.)

**NUTRITION
PROFESSIONAL:**
Is there anyone you
would like to be
with us as we talk,
and do you mind
them hearing our
conversation?

NUTRICIONISTA:
*¿Hay alguien que le gustaría tener
con nosotros mientras hablamos,
y le importa si escucha nuestra
conversación?*
(ay AHL-gee-ehn keh leh goos-
tah-REE-ah teh-NEHR kohn
noh-SOH-trohs mee-EHN-trahs
ah-BLAH-mohs, ee leh eem-POHR-
tah see ehs-KOO-chah noo-EHS-trah
kohn-behr-sah-see-OHN?)

CLIENT:
My husband came
with me. I do not
mind if he hears us.

CLIENTE:
*Mi esposo vino conmigo. Él puede
escuchar la conversación.*
(mee ehs-POH-soh BEE-no kohn-
MEE-go. ehl PWEH-theh ehs-KOO-
chahr lah kohn-behr-sah-see-OHN.)

**NUTRITION
PROFESSIONAL:**
Great! And how
many others are in
your family?

NUTRICIONISTA:
*Excelente. ¿Y cuántos más hay en su
familia?*
(ehk-seh-LEHN-teh. ee KWOHN-tohs
mahs ay ehn soo fah-MEE-lee-ah?)

CLIENT:
Three children and my mother-in-law live with us.

CLIENTE:
Tenemos tres hijos y mi suegra también vive con nosotros.
(teh-NEH-mohs trehs EE-hohs ee mee SWEH-grah tahm-bee-EHN BEE-beh kohn noh-SOH-trohs.)

NUTRITION PROFESSIONAL:
Who does the cooking for the family?

NUTRICIONISTA:
¿Quién prepara la comida para la familia?
(kee-EHN preh-PAH-rah lah koh-MEE-thah PAH-rah lah fah-MEE-lee-ah?)

CLIENT:
I do the cooking.

CLIENTE:
Yo cocino.
(yoh koh-SEE-noh.)

NUTRITION PROFESSIONAL:
I'd like to talk with you about cooking, but there are other questions I'd like to ask first. Will that be fine with you?

NUTRICIONISTA:
Me gustaría hablar con usted sobre la cocina, pero tengo unas cuantas preguntas primero. ¿Está bien?
(meh goos-tah-REE-ah ah-BLAHR kohn oo-STEHD SOH-breh la koh-SEE-nah, PEH-roh TEHN-goh OO-nahs KWAHN-tahs preh-GOON-tahs pree-MEH-roh. Eh-STAH bee-EHN?)

CLIENT:
Yes, that is fine.

CLIENTE:
Sí, está bien.
(see eh-STAH bee-EHN.)

NUTRITION PROFESSIONAL:
If there are any questions you do not want to answer, please let me know. We have about an hour. Do you have any questions before I begin?

NUTRICIONISTA:
Si hay alguna pregunta que no le gustaría contestar, por favor hágamelo saber. Tenemos aproximadamente una hora. ¿Tiene usted cualquier pregunta antes de que empecemos?
(see ay ahl-GOON-ah preh-GOON-tah keh noh leh goos-tah-REE-ah kohn-tehs-TAHR, pohr fah-BOHR AH-gah-meh-loh sah-BEHR. teh-NEH-mohs ah-prohk-see-mah-thah-MEHN-teh OO-nah OH-rah. tee-EH-neh oo-STEHD kwahl-kee-EHR preh-GOON-tah AHN-tehs deh keh ehm-peh-SEH-mohs?)

CLIENT:
No, I don't have any questions.

CLIENTE:
No, no tengo preguntas.
(noh, noh TEHN-goh preh-GOON-tahs.)

NUTRITION PROFESSIONAL:
Your doctor has asked me to talk to you about the food you eat. Did your doctor talk to you about a special diet?

NUTRICIONISTA:
Su médico me ha pedido que hable con usted sobre los alimentos que come. ¿Le habló su médico de una dieta especial?
(soo MEH-dee-koh meh ah peh-DEE-thoh keh AH-bleh kohn oo-STEHD SOH-breh lohs ah-lee-MEHN-tohs keh KOH-meh. leh ah-BLOH soo MEH-dee-koh deh OO-nah dee-EH-tah ehs-peh-see-AHL?)

CLIENT:
I do not remember what he said.

CLIENTE:
No recuerdo lo que me dijo.
(noh rreh-KWEHR-doh loh keh meh DEE-hoh.)

Spanish Basics

NUTRITION PROFESSIONAL:
Your doctor wants you to learn about a diet for managing diabetes. Before we talk about that diet, I'd like to ask about your meals.

NUTRICIONISTA:
Su médico quisiera que aprenda sobre una dieta para la diabetes. Antes de hablar de la dieta, primero me gustaría preguntarle sobre sus comidas.
(soo MEH-dee-koh kee-see-EH-rah keh ah-PREHN-dah SOH-breh OO-nah dee-EH-tah PAH-rah lah dee-ah-BEH-tehs. AHN-tehs deh ah-BLAHR deh la dee-EH-tah, pree-MEH-ro meh goos-tah-REE-ah preh-goon-TAHR-leh SOH-breh soos koh-MEE-thahs.)

CLIENT:
OK.

CLIENTE:
Está bien.
(ehs-TAH bee-EHN.)

NUTRITION PROFESSIONAL:
What time do you eat your first meal?

NUTRICIONISTA:
Señora Mendoza, ¿cuándo come usted su primera comida del día?
(sehn-YOH-rah Mehn-DOH-sah, KWAHN-doh KOH-meh oo-STEHD soo pree-MEH-rah koh-MEE-thah dehl DEE-ah?)

CLIENT:
Usually I eat breakfast at 8:00 AM.

CLIENTE:
Como el desayuno a las ocho de la mañana.
(KOH-moh ehl deh-sah-YOO-noh ah lahs OH-choh de lah mahn-YAH-nah.)

NUTRITION PROFESSIONAL:
And what time do you usually eat your next meals?

NUTRICIONISTA:
¿Y a qué hora come las otras comidas?
(ee ah keh OH-rah KOH-meh lahs OH-trahs koh-MEE-thahs?)

CLIENT:
I generally eat lunch at 12:30, and dinner at 7:00.

CLIENTE:
Generalmente como el almuerzo a las doce y media, y la cena a las siete.
(heh-neh-rahl-MEHN-te KOH-moh ehl ahl-MWEHR-soh ah lahs doh-seh ee MEH-thee-yah, ee lah SEH-nah ah lahs see-YEH-teh.)

NUTRITION PROFESSIONAL:
Do you eat a snack?

NUTRICIONISTA:
¿Come usted una merienda?
(KOH-meh oo-STEHD OO-nah meh-ree-YEN-dah?)

CLIENT:
Yes, I eat a snack at around 4:30.

CLIENTE:
Sí, como una merienda a las cuatro y media, más o menos.
(see, KOH-moh OO-nah meh-ree-YEN-dah a lahs KWAH-troh ee MEH-thee-yah, mahs oh meh-nohs.)

After practicing this dialogue a few times, try to write your own dialogue. You might add some of the basic vocabulary you previously learned. Find a partner to help you practice, then try having an impromptu conversation.

CHAPTER 12

Breakfast Foods

English	Español	Pronunciation
artificial sweetener	*endulzante (artificial)*	ehn-dool-SAHN-teh (ahr-tee-fee-see-AHL)
avocado	*aguacate*	ah-gwah-KAH-teh
	palta	PAHL-tah
bacon	*tocino*	toh-SEE-noh
	tocineta	toh-see-NEH-tah
	panceta	pahn-SEH-tah
beans (dried, canned, or cooked, usually black)	*frijoles*	free-HOH-lehs
	habichuelas	ah-bee-CHWEH-lahs
	porotos	poh-ROH-tohs
bread (*see also* toast)	*pan*	pahn

English	Español	Pronunciation
wheat bread	*pan de trigo*	pahn deh TREE-goh
white bread	*pan blanco*	pahn BLAHN-koh
whole grain bread	*pan integral*	pahn een-teh-GRAHL[b]
bread roll	*bolillo*	boh-LEE-yoh
	panecillo	pah-neh-SEE-yoh
butter (can also refer to lard)	*mantequilla*	mahn-teh-KEE-yah
	manteca	mahn-TEH-kah
cereal	*cereal*	seh-reh-AHL
	maizoro	mah-ee-SOH-roh
cheese	*queso*	KEH-soh
coffee	*café*	kah-FEH
coffee with milk	*café con leche*	kah-FEH kohn LEH-cheh
cream	*nata*	NAH-tah
eggs	*huevos*[a]	WEH-bohs
	blanquillos	blahn-KEE-yohs
eggs, scrambled	*huevos revueltos*	WEH-bohs rreh-BWEHL-tohs

---

[a] Pan integral is *often pronounced as one word, pah-neen-teh-grahl.*

[b] *Some cultures consider the word* huevos *to be obscene when used in any context not referring to food. However, the majority of Spanish-speaking individuals equate this term with eggs.*

English	Español	Pronunciation
egg white	*clara de huevo*	KLAH-rah deh WEH-boh
	clara de blanquillo	KLAH-rah deh blahn-KEE-yoh
egg yolk	*yema de huevo*	YEH-mah deh WEH-boh
	yema de blanquillo	YEH-mah deh blahn-KEE-yoh
egg omelet	*tortilla francesa*	tohr-TEE-ya frahn-SEH-sah
	tortilla de huevo	tohr-TEE-ya deh WEH-boh
french toast	*tostada francesa*	tohs-TAH-thah frahn-SEH-sah
	torrija	toh-rree-hah
	torreja	toh-rreh-hah
fruits	*frutas*	FROO-tahs
ham	*jamón*	hah-MOHN
hash browns[c]	*papas doradas*	PAH-pahs doh-rah-thahs
honey	*miel de abeja*	mee-YEHL deh ah-BEH-hah

---

[c] *Onions are often added to potatoes.*

English	Español	Pronunciation
jelly[d]	jalea	hah-LEH-yah
	mermelada	mehr-meh-LAH-thah
	dulce	DOOL-seh
	ate	AH-teh
juice	jugo	HOO-goh
	zumo	THOO-moh
apple juice	jugo de manzana	HOO-goh deh mahn-SAH-nah
cranberry juice	jugo de arándano agrio	HOO-goh deh ah-RAHN-dah-noh AH-gree-yoh
grape juice	jugo de uva	HOO-goh deh OO-bah
orange juice	jugo de naranja	HOO-goh deh nah-RAHN-hah
	jugo de china	HOO-goh deh CHEE-nah
tomato juice	jugo de tomate	HOO-goh deh toh-MAH-teh
	jugo de jitomate	HOO-go deh hee-toh-MAH-teh

[d] Ate *is frequently made from quince or guava.* Jalea *usually has no pulp, whereas* mermelada *contains pulp and/or seeds.*

English	Español	Pronunciation
margarine	*margarina*	mahr-gah-REE-nah
	aceite vegetal hidrogenado	ah-SEH-ee-teh beh-heh-TAHL ee-droh-heh-NAH-thoh
milk	*leche*	LEH-cheh
chocolate milk	*leche de chocolate*	LEH-cheh deh choh-koh-LAH-teh
evaporated milk	*leche evaporada*	LEH-cheh eh-bah-poh-RAH-thah
sweetened condensed milk	*leche condensada*	LEH-cheh kohn-dehn-SAH-thah
oatmeal	*avena*	ah-BEH-nah
pancakes	*panqueques*	pahn-KEH-kehs
	panques	PAHN-kehs
	crepas	KREH-pahs
	panquecas	pahn-KEH-kahs
	hotcakes	HOHT-kehks
pastry	*pan dulce*[e]	pahn DOOL-seh

[e] *This is usually a sweet bread instead of a rich pastry.*

Breakfast

English	Español	Pronunciation
plantain	*plátano*	PLAH-tah-noh
	plátano macho	PLAH-tah-noh MAH-choh
	plátano grande	PLAH-tah-noh GRAHN-deh
sausage	*salchicha*	sahl-CHEE-chah
	chorizo	choh-REE-soh
sugar	*azúcar*	ah-SOO-kahr
syrup	*almíbar*	ahl-MEE-bahr
	sirope	see-ROH-peh
	jarabe	ha-RAH-beh
tea	*té*	teh
toast	*pan tostado*	pahn toh-STAH-thoh
	tostadas	tohs-TAH-thahs
white toast	*pan blanco tostado*	pahn BLAHN-koh toh-STAH-thoh
wheat toast	*pan de trigo tostado*	pahn deh TREE-go toh-STAH-thoh

English	Español	Pronunciation
whole grain toast	*pan integral*[a] *tostado*	pahn een-teh-GRAHL toh-STAH-thoh
tortilla	*tortilla*[f]	tohr-TEE-yah
corn tortilla	*tortilla de maiz*	tohr-TEE-yah deh mah-EES
flour tortilla	*tortilla de harina*	tohr-TEE-yah deh ah-REE-nah
waffles	*wafles*	WAH-flehs
yogurt	*yogur*	yoh-GOOR

Breakfast

[a] Pan integral is *often pronounced as one word, pah-neen-teh-grahl.*

[f] *In Spain and some South American countries, a* tortilla *is an egg and potato torte, not a type of bread.*

CHAPTER 13

Lunch and Dinner Foods

In Latino culture, lunch is the main meal and dinner may consists of leftovers from lunch. Therefore, many of the foods in this section are eaten for both lunch and dinner. For this reason, they appear together in this chapter. The foods are grouped in two lists: The first gives English and Spanish words for common foods; the second provides Latino foods that have no unique English name (such as *burrito* or *sopes*) and gives a description of each item.

English to Spanish Translations

English	Español	Pronunciation
appetizer	*antojito*	ahn-toh-HEE-toh
	aperitivo	ah-peh-ree-TEE-boh
	entrada	ehn-TRAH-thah
barbecued meat	*barbacoa*	bahr-bah-KOH-ah
	picada	pee-KAH-thah
beef	*carne de res*	KAHR-neh deh RREHS
	carne roja	KAHR-neh RROH-hah
grilled beef	*carne asada*	KAHR-neh ah-SAH-thah
	carne a la tampiqueña	KAHR-neh ah lah tahm-pee-KEHN-yah
	carne a la plancha	KAHR-neh ah lah PLAHN-chah
ground beef	*carne molida*	KAHR-neh moh-LEE-thah
	carne picada	KAHR-neh pee-KAH-thah
bread	*pan*	pahn
cheese	*queso*	KEH-soh
chicken	*pollo*	POH-yoh

English	Español	Pronunciation
chili with meat	*chile con carne*[a]	CHEE-leh kohn KAHR-neh
chips (snack chips)	*chips*	cheeps
	totopos	toh-TOH-pohs
	papitas de bolsa	pah-PEE-tahs deh BOHL-sah
	papitas fritas	pah-PEE-tahs FREE-tahs
	tostaditas	toh-stah-THEE-tahs
cold cuts	*carne para sándwich*	KAHR-neh pah-rah SAHND-weech
	embutidos	ehm-boo-TEE-thohs
cole slaw	*ensalada de col*	ehn-sah-LAH-thah deh KOHL
	ensalada de repollo	ehn-sah-LAH-thah deh rreh-POH-yoh
duck	*pato*	PAH-toh
fish	*pescado*	peh-SKAH-thoh
clams	*almejas*	ahl-MEH-hahs

Lunch and Dinner

---
[a] Con carne is *often pronounced as one word, kohn-KAHR-neh.*

English	Español	Pronunciation
lobster	*langosta*	lahn-GOH-stah
octopus	*pulpo*	POOL-poh
oysters	*ostiones*	oh-stee-YOH-nehs
shellfish	*mariscos*	mah-REE-skohs
shrimp	*camarón*	kah-mah-ROHN
squid	*calamar*	kah-lah-MAHR
tuna	*atún*	ah-TOON
french fries	*papas fritas*	PAH-pahs FREE-tahs
	papitas	pah-PEE-tahs
ham	*jamón*	hah-MOHN
hamburger	*hamburguesa*	ahm-boor-GEH-sah
hash (with meat)	*picadillo*	pee-kah-DEE-yoh
heart	*corazón*	koh-rah-SOHN
hot dog	*salchicha*	sahl-CHEE-chah
	hot dog	HOHT dohg
	pancho	PAHN-choh

English	Español	Pronunciation
ketchup[b]	*catsup*	KAHT-soop
	salsa de tomate	SAHL-sah deh toh-MAH-teh
	salsa de jitomate	SAHL-sah deh hee- toh-MAH-teh
kidneys	*riñones*	rreen-YOH-nehs
lamb	*cordero*	kohr-THEH-roh
	carnero	kahr-NEH-roh
lentils	*lentejas*	lehn-TEH-hahs
liver	*hígado*	EE-gah-thoh
mayonnaise	*mayonesa*	mah-yoh-NEE-sah
meatballs	*albóndigas*	ahl-BOHN-dee-gahs
mustard	*mostaza*	moh-STAH-sah
noodles (thin pasta, vermicelli)	*fideos*	fee-THEH-yohs
pork skins, fried	*chicharrones*	chee-cha-RROHN-ehs

[b] *These terms are also used for tomato sauce.*

English	Español	Pronunciation
peanut butter	*crema de cacahuate*	KREH-mah deh kah-kah-WAH-teh
	crema de maní	KREH-mah deh mah-NEE
	mantequilla de cacahuate	mahn-teh-KEE-ya deh kah-kah-WAH-teh
	mantequilla de maní	mahn-teh-KEE-ya deh mah-NEE
	manteca de maní	mahn-TEH-kah deh mah-NEE
peppers, stuffed	*chiles rellenos*	CHEE-lehs rreh-YEH-nohs
	ajíes rellenos	ah-HEE-yehs rreh-YEH-nohs
	pimientos rellenos	pee-mee-YEHN-tohs rreh-YEH-nohs
pizza	*pizza*	PEET-sah
popcorn	*palomitas (de maíz)*	pah-loh-MEE-tahs (deh mah-EES)
pork	*puerco*	PWEHR-koh
	cerdo	SEHR-thoh

English	Español	Pronunciation
pork chop	*chuleta de puerco*	choo-LEH-tah deh PWEHR-koh
	chuleta de cerdo	choo-LEH-tah deh SEHR-thoh
	costilla de ceroso	koh-STEE-yah deh seh-ROH-soh
	costilla de cerdo	koh-STEE-yah deh SEHR-thoh
pretzel	*prétzel*	PREHT-sehl
refried beans	*frijoles refritos*	free-HOH-lehs rreh-FREE-tohs
rice	*arroz*	ah-RROHS
salad	*ensalada*	ehn-sah-LAH-thah
salad dressing	*aderezo*	ah-deh-REH-soh
	aliño	ah-LEEN-yoh
	condimento	kohn-dee-MEHN-toh
saltines/ crackers	*galletas saladas*	gah-YEH-tahs sah-LAH-thahs
	galletitas de agua	gah-yeh-TEE-tahs deh AH-gwah

English	Español	Pronunciation
sandwich	*sándwich*	SAHND-weech
	torta	TOHR-tah
	bocadillo[c]	boh-kah-DEE-yoh
	emparedado	ehm-pah-reh-THAH-thoh
[type of] sandwich	*sándwich de* [type]	SAHND-weech deh [type]
grilled cheese sandwich	*sándwich de queso fundido*	SAHND-weech deh KEH-soh foon-DEE-thoh
	sándwich de queso derretido	SAHND-weech deh KEH-soh deh-rreh-TEE-thoh
sauce (or paste)	*mole* (a Mexican sauce)	MOH-leh
	salsa	SAHL-sah
soft drink	*refresco*	rreh-FREHS-koh
	gaseosa	gah-seh-OH-sah
	soda	SOH-thah

Lunch and Dinner

---

[c] Bocadillo *may also refer to a snack or appetizer.*

English	Español	Pronunciation
diet soft drink	*refresco de dieta*	rreh-FREHS-koh deh dee-EH-tah
	gaseosa de dieta	gah-seh-OH-sah deh dee-EH-tah
	refresco lite	rreh-FREHS-koh LAHYT
	gaseosa lite	gah-seh-OH-sah LAHYT
soup[c]	*sopa*	SOH-pah
	caldo	KAHL-doh
spaghetti	*espaguetis/ espaguettis*	eh-spah-GEH-tees
steak	*bistec*	BEE-stehk or bee-STEHK
	bife	BEE-feh
	guisado	ghee-SAH-thoh
skirt steak	*fajita*	fah-HEE-tah
sweetbreads/ gizzards	*mollejas*	moh-YEH-hahs

[d] *In northern Mexico,* sopa *may also refer to a dish with pasta and tomatoes.* Caldo *is also used for broth.*

English	Español	Pronunciation
tripe	*tripas*	TREE-pahs
turkey	*pavo*	PAH-boh
	guajolote[e]	gwah-hoh-LOH-teh
water	*agua*	AH-gwah
flavored water	*agua saborizada*	AH-gwah sah-boh-ree-SAH-thah
	agua de sabor	AH-gwah deh sah-BOHR
mineral water	*agua mineral*	AH-gwah mee-neh-RAHL
sparkling water	*agua con gas*	AH-gwah kohn GAHS
	agua gasificada	AH-gwah gah-see-fee-KAH-thah
	agua mineral	AH-gwah mee-neh-RAHL
yogurt	*yogur*	yoh-GOOR

[e] *Some people use* guajolote *to refer only to a live turkey.*

Latino Foods Without English Translations

The following is a selection of popular Latino foods that have no English translations. When discussing these foods with your clients, it is advisable to use the Spanish terms even if the conversation is in English.

Español	Pronunciation	Description
burrito/burro	boo-RREE-toh/ BOO-rroh	filled tortilla
carnitas	kahr-NEE-tahs	shredded pork
ceviche	seh-BEE-cheh	raw seafood salad
chile con queso	CHEE-leh kohn KEH-soh	cheese dip
chimichanga	chee-mee-CHAHN-gah	deep-fried filled burrito
empanada	ehm-pah-NAH-thah	pie filled with meat, vegetables, or fruit
enchilada	ehn-chee-LAH-thah	filled tortilla, with sauce and cheese
envueltos	ehn-BWEHL-tohs	fried tacos
gazpacho	gahs-PAH-choh	cold soup with tomatoes and vegetables

Lunch and Dinner

Español	Pronunciation	Description
guacamole	gwah-kah-MOH-leh	avocado dip
licuado	lee-KWAH-thoh	pureed fruit drink of water, ice, and sugar, sometimes with milk and a raw egg
		To describe the type of drink, one would say *licuado de* ... followed by the fruit. For example, *licuado de fresa* (lee-KWAH-thoh deh FREH-sah) is made with strawberries; *licuado de piña* (lee-KWAH-thoh deh PEEN-yah) is made with pineapple.
pastel de carne	pahs-TEHL deh KAHR-neh	meat pie
quesadilla	keh-sah-DEE-yah	tortillas filled with cheese, and sometimes meat, poultry, and/or vegetables
salsa	SAHL-sah	tomato-based dip/sauce
sopes	SOH-pehs	corn-dough bowls, filled with beans, sauce, and cheese

Español	Pronunciation	Description
tamales	tah-MAH-lehs	corn husk or plantain leaves stuffed with corn dough and other fillings
tortilla	tohr-TEE-yah	flat bread made from wheat or corn
tostada	toh-STAH-thah	fried tortilla, with beans, meat, or vegetables

CHAPTER 14

Vegetables

English	Español	Pronunciation
beet	*remolacha*	rreh-moh-LAH-chah
	betabel	beh-tah-BEHL
broccoli	*broccoli*	BROH-koh-lee
	brécol	BREH-kohl
brussels sprouts	*col de Bruselas*	kohl deh broo-SEH-lahs
	bruselas	broo-SEH-lahs
	repollitos de Bruselas	rreh-poh-YEE-tohs deh broo-SEH-lahs
	colecitas de Bruselas	koh-leh-SEE-tahs deh broo-SEH-lahs
cabbage	*col*	kohl
	repollo	rreh-POH-yoh

English	Español	Pronunciation
cactus	*nopal*	noh-PAHL
	nopalitos	noh-pah-LEE-tohs
carrots	*zanahorias*	sah-nah-OH-ree-yahs
cauliflower	*coliflor*	koh-lee-FLOHR
celery	*apio*	AH-pee-oh
chili pepper	*chile*	CHEE-leh
specific types of chiles	*jalapeño* (small, hot)	hah-lah-PEHN-yoh
	chipotle (smoked jalapeño)	chee-POHT-leh
	serrano (small, hot)	seh-RRAH-noh
	habañero (small, hot)	ah-bahn-YEH-roh
	poblano (larger, mild)	poh-BLAH-noh
	ají	ah-HEE
corn	*maíz*	mah-EES
	elote	eh-LOH-teh

English	Español	Pronunciation
corn husk (used for tamales)	*oja*	OH-hah
	hoja de maíz	OH-hah theh mah-EES
	hoja	OH-hah
corn on the cob	*elote*	eh-LOH-teh
	mazorca de maíz	mah-SOHR-kah deh mah-EES
	choclo de maíz	CHOH-kloh deh mah-EES
cucumber	*pepino*	peh-PEE-noh
dark-green leafy vegetables	*verduras de hojas verdes*	behr-DOO-rahs deh OH-hahs BEHR-dehs
eggplant	*berenjena*	beh-rehn-HEH-nah
green beans	*judías verdes*	hoo-THEE-ahs BEHR-dehs
	ejotes	eh-HOH-tehs
	porotos verdes	poh-ROH-tehs BEHR-dehs
	habichuelas verdes	ah-bee-CHWEH-lahs BEHR-dehs

Vegetables and Fruits

English	Español	Pronunciation
green bell pepper	*pimiento verde*	pee-mee-EHN-toh BEHR-deh
	chile verde	CHEE-leh BEHR-deh
	aji verde	ah-HEE BEHR-deh
	chile ancho	CHEE-leh AHN-choh
	pimiento dulce	pee-mee-EHN-toh DOOL-seh
green peas	*guisantes*	ghee-SAHN-tehs
	chícharos	CHEE-chah-rohs
	petit pois	peh-tee PWAH
jicama (a white-fleshed root vegetable)	*jícama*	HEE-kah-mah
leek	*puerro*	PWEH-rroh
lettuce	*lechuga*	leh-CHOO-gah
mushroom	*hongo*	OHN-goh
	champiñón	chahm-peen-YOHN

English	Español	Pronunciation
okra	*quingombó*	keen-gohm-BOH
	calabú	kah-lah-BOO
	quimbombó	keem-bohm-BOH
onion	*cebolla*	seh-BOH-yah
green onion/ scallion	*cebolla de verdeo*	seh-BOH-yah deh behr-THEH-oh
	cebolla larga	seh-BOH-yah LAHR-gah
	cebolleta	seh-BOH-YEH-tah
shallots	*chalotes*	chah-LOH-tehs
	chalotas	chah-LOH-tahs
potatoes	*papas*	PAH-pahs
	patatas	pah-TAH-tahs
pumpkin	*calabaza*	cah-lah-BAH-sah
radish	*rábano*	RRAH-bah-noh
spinach	*espinacas*	eh-spee-NAH-kahs
	espinaca	eh-spee-NAH-kah

Vegetables and Fruits

English	Español	Pronunciation
sweet potatoes	*batatas*	bah-TAH-tahs
	camotes	kah-MOH-tehs
	boniatos	boh-nee-YAH-tohs
tomatillo (husk tomato; looks like a small green tomato)	*tomatillo*	toh-mah-TEE-yoh
tomato	*tomate*	toh-MAH-teh
	jitomate	hee-toh-MAH-teh
turnip	*nabo*	NAH-boh
zucchini	*calabacita*	kah-lah-bah-SEE-tah
	calabacín	kah-lah-bah-SEEN
	zapallito	sah-pah-YEE-toh

CHAPTER 15

Fruit

English	Español	Pronunciation
apple	*manzana*	mahn-SAH-nah
apricot	*albaricoque*	ahl-bah-ree-KOH-keh
	damasco	dah-MAHS-koh
	chabacano	chah-bah-KAH-noh
banana	*plátano*	PLAH-tah-noh
	banana	bah-NAH-nah
	banano	bah-NAH-noh
	guineo	ghee-NEH-oh
blackberry	*mora*	MOH-rah
blueberries	*arándanos (azules)*	ah-RAHN-dah-nohs (ah-SOO-lehs)

Vegetables and Fruits

English	Español	Pronunciation
cantaloupe	*cantalupo*	kahn-tah-LOO-poh
	melón	meh-LOHN
cherries	*cerezas*	seh-REH-sahs
coconut	*coco*	KOH-koh
cranberries	*arándanos rojos (y agrios)*	ah-RAHN-dah-nohs RROH-hohs (ee AH-gree-ohs)
date	*dátil*	DAH-teel
fig	*higo*	EE-goh
grapefruit	*toronja*	toh-ROHN-hah
	pomelo	poh-MEH-loh
grapes	*uvas*	OO-bahs
guava (similar to a peach)	*guava*	GWAH-bah
	guayaba/ guayava	gwah-YAH-bah
kiwi	*kiwi*	KEE-wee
lemon/lime[a]	*limón*	lee-MOHN
	lima	LEE-mah

[a] *The Spanish words for lemon and lime vary from country to country; sometimes* lima *refers to lemon and* limón *refers to lime.*

English	Español	Pronunciation
mango	*mango*	MAHN-goh
nectarine	*nectarina*	nehk-tah-REE-nah
	pelón	peh-LOHN
orange	*naranja*	nah-RAHN-hah
	china	CHEE-nah
papaya	*papaya*	pah-PAH-yah
	fruta bomba	FROO-tah BOHM-bah
passion fruit	*granadilla*	grah-nah-DEE-yah
	maracuyá	mah-rah-koo-YAH
	parcha	PAHR-chah
peach	*durazno*	doo-RAHS-noh
	melocotón	meh-loh-koh-TOHN
pear	*pera*	PEH-rah
pineapple	*piña*	PEEN-yah
	ananá	ah-nah-NAH
plum	*ciruela*	seer-WEH-lah
pomegranate	*granada*	grah-NAH-thah

Vegetables and Fruits

English	Español	Pronunciation
prunes	*ciruelas pasas*	seer-WEH-lahs PAH-sahs
	pasas	PAH-sahs
	pasas de uva	PAH-sahs deh OO-bah
raisins	*uvas pasas*	OO-bahs PAH-sahs
raspberries	*frambuesas*	frahm-BWEH-sahs
strawberries	*fresas*	FREH-sahs
	frutillas	froo-TEE-yahs
tangerine	*mandarina*	mahn-dah-REE-nah
watermelon	*sandía*	sahn-DEE-yah
	patilla	pah-TEE-yah

CHAPTER 16

Desserts and Sweets

The foods in this chapter are grouped into two lists: The first provides English to Spanish translations; the second includes Latino desserts that have no unique English name (such as *churro*). This second list provides a description of each food.

English to Spanish Translations

English	Español	Pronunciation
cake	*pastel*	pah-STEHL
	torta	TOHR-tah
	bizcocho[a]	bees-KOH-choh

---

[a] Bizcocho is the word most commonly used for cake in the Caribbean. In Mexico, bizcochito is often considered obscene.

English	Español	Pronunciation
candy; sweets	*dulces*	DOOL-sehs
	caramelos	kah-rah-MEH-lohs
	golosinas	goh-loh-SEE-nahs
chocolate or hot chocolate	*chocolate*[b]	choh-koh-LAH-teh
cookies	*galletas (dulces)*	gah-YEH-tahs (DOOL-sehs)
cupcake	*pastelito*	pahs-teh-LEE-toh
	magdalena	mahg-dah-LEH-nah
	cubilete	koo-bee-LEH-teh
	mantecada	mahn-teh-KAH-thah
	pastelillo	pahs-teh-LEE-yoh
	bizcochito[a]	bees-koh-CHEE-toh
custard	*flan*	flahn
donuts	*donas*	DOH-nahs
	rosquillas[c]	rroh-SKEE-yahs

---

[a] Bizcocho *is the word most commonly used for* cake *in the Caribbean. In Mexico,* bizcochito *is often considered obscene.*

[b] *When describing a chocolate-flavored food, use* [type of food] de chocolate *(deh choh-koh-LAH-teh). For example,* pastel de chocolate *(pah-STEHL deh choh-koh-LAH-teh) translates as* chocolate cake.

[c] *In Honduras,* rosquillas *are made from a pretzel-shaped, salty-sweet cheese dough that is baked until hard and crispy.*

English	Español	Pronunciation
gelatin	*gelatina*	heh-lah-TEE-nah
ice cream	*helado*	eh-LAH-thoh
	nieve	nee-EH-beh
	mantecado	mahn-teh-KAH-thoh
muffin	*panque*	PAHN-keh
	panecillo	pah-neh-SEE-yoh
	mollete	moh-YEH-teh
	muffin	MOH-feen
pie	*pai*	PAH-ee
	pastel	pah-STEHL
	empanada	ehm-pah-NAH-thah
	tarta	TAHR-tah
	torta	TOHR-tah
pudding	*pudín*	poo-THEEN
shaved ice, with flavored syrup	*raspado*	rrah-SPAH-thoh
	piraguas	pee-RAH-gwahs

Other Foods and Drinks

English	Español	Pronunciation
sherbet/sorbet	*sorbete*	sohr-BEH-teh
	helado de nieve	eh-LAH-thoh deh nee-eh-beh
	helado de agua	eh-LAH-thoh deh AH-gwah
sweets	*dulces*	DOOL-sehs

Other Foods and Drinks

Latino Sweets Without English Translations

The following is a selection of popular Latino desserts and sweets that have no English translations. When discussing these foods with your clients, it is advisable to use the Spanish terms even if the conversation is in English.

Español	Pronunciation	Description
buñuelo	boon-yoo-EH-loh	pastry, deep-fried
churro	CHOO-rroh	sweet dough, deep-fried
leche quemada	LEH-cheh keh-MAH-thah	candy made with goat's milk

CHAPTER 17

Beverages

The beverages in this chapter are grouped in three lists: The first provides English to Spanish translations for common beverages; the second describes types of milk; and the third includes Latino beverages that have no unique English name (such as *horchata*). This final list provides descriptions of each drink.

English to Spanish Translations

English	Español	Pronunciation
beer	*cerveza*	sehr-BEH-sah
coffee	*café*	kah-FEH
coffee with milk (and sugar)	*café con leche*	kah-FEH kohn LEH-cheh
drink/beverage	*bebida*[a]	beh-BEE-thah

[a] *This sometimes indicates an alcoholic drink.*

English	Español	Pronunciation
iced tea	*té helado*	teh eh-LAH-thoh
	té frío[a]	teh FREE-oh
juice	*jugo*	HOO-goh
apple juice	*jugo de manzana*	HOO-goh deh mahn-SAH-nah
cranberry juice	*jugo de arándano agrio*	HOO-goh deh ah-RAHN-dah-noh AH-gree-yoh
fruit juice	*jugo de frutas*	HOO-goh deh FROO-tahs
grape juice	*jugo de uva*	HOO-goh deh OO-bah
orange juice	*jugo de naranja*	HOO-goh deh nah-RAHN-hah
	jugo de china	HOO-goh deh CHEE-nah
tomato juice	*jugo de tomate*	HOO-goh deh toh-MAH-teh
	jugo de jitomate	HOO-goh deh hee-toh-MAH-teh

[a]   Té frío i*s often pronounced as one word,* teh-FREE-oh.

English	Español	Pronunciation
vegetable juice	*jugo de vegetales*	HOO-goh deh beh-heh-TAH-lehs
	jugo de verduras	HOO-goh deh behr-DOO-rahs
	v ocho (ie, V8 Juices [Campbell Soup Co, Camden, NJ])	beh-oh-choh
lemonade	*limonada*	lee-moh-NAH-thah
milkshake	*batido*	bah-TEE-thoh
	licuado	lee-KWAH-thoh
soft drink	*refresco*	rreh-FREHS-koh
	gaseosa	gah-seh-OH-sah
	soda	SOH-thah
diet soft drink	*refresco de dieta*	rreh-FREHS-koh deh dee-EH-tah
	gaseosa de dieta	gah-seh-OH-sah deh dee-EH-tah
	refresco lite	rreh-FREHS-koh LAYT
	gaseosa lite	gah-seh-OH-sah LAYT

Other Foods and Drinks

English	Español	Pronunciation
tea	*té*	teh
water	*agua*	AH-gwah
whiskey	*whiskey/ güisqui*	WEES-kee
wine	*vino*	BEE-noh
red wine	*vino tinto*	BEE-noh TEEN-toh
	vino rojo	BEE-noh RROH-hoh
white wine	*vino blanco*	BEE-noh BLAHN-koh

Varieties of Milk: English to Spanish Translations

English	Español	Pronunciation
buttermilk	*suero*	SWEH-roh
cream	*crema*	KREH-mah
	nata	NAH-tah
chocolate milk	*leche de chocolate*	LEH-cheh deh choh-koh-LAH-teh
	leche chocolate	LEH-cheh choh-koh-LAH-teh

English	Español	Pronunciation
chocolate milk (*cont.*)	*leche con Quik* (Nestlé Nesquik [Nestlé, Vevey, Switzerland])	LEH-cheh kohn KWEEK
	leche achocolatada	LEH-cheh ah-choh-koh-lah-TAH-thah
coconut milk	*leche de coco*	LEH-cheh deh KOH-koh
evaporated milk	*leche evaporada*	LEH-cheh eh-bah-poh-RAH-thah
low-fat milk[a]	*leche de un porciento*	LEH-cheh deh oon pohr-see-EHN-toh
	leche descremada	LEH-cheh dehs-kreh-MAH-thah
nonfat (skim) milk[a]	*leche sin grasa*	LEH-cheh seen GRAH-sah
	leche desgrasada	LEH-cheh dehs-grah-SAH-thah
	leche descremada	LEH-cheh dehs-kreh-MAH-thah
powdered milk	*leche en polvo*	LEH-cheh ehn POHL-boh

Other Foods and Drinks

---

[a] *Many Spanish-speaking countries only offer whole milk, low-fat milk (usually 1.5% fat), and nonfat milk.*

English	Español	Pronunciation
reduced-fat (2%) milk[a]	*leche de dos porciento*	LEH-cheh deh dohs pohr-see-EHN-toh
sweetened condensed milk	*leche condensada*	LEH-cheh kohn-dehn-SAH-thah
whole milk[a]	*leche entera*	LEH-cheh ehn-TEH-rah
	leche sin descremar	LEH-cheh seen dehs-kreh-MAHR

[a]   *Many Spanish-speaking countries only offer whole milk, low-fat milk (usually 1.5% fat), and nonfat milk.*

Latino Beverages Without English Translations

The following is a selection of popular Latino beverages that have no English translations. When discussing these foods with your clients, it is advisable to use the Spanish terms even if the conversation is in English.

Español	Pronunciation	Description
agua de frutas	AH-gwah deh FROO-tahs	fruit drink (made with pureed fruit, water, sugar, and ice)
agua de horchata	AH-gwah deh ohr-CHAH-tah	See *horchata,* below.
horchata	ohr-CHAH-tah	rice water; often includes milk, sugar, cinnamon, and sometimes other starches
licuado	lee-KWAH-thoh	pureed fruit drink of water, ice, and sugar, sometimes with milk and a raw egg *To describe the type of drink, one would say* licuado de . . . *followed by the fruit. For example,* licuado de fresa *(lee-KWAH-thoh deh FREH-sah) is made with strawberries; a* licuado de piña *(lee-KWAH-thoh deh PEEN-yah) is made with pineapple.*
sangría	sahn-GREE-yah	red or white wine drink with sugar and fruit
tequila	teh-KEE-lah	liquor, distilled, from the agave plant

Other Foods and Drinks

CHAPTER 18

Additional Foods

Cheese

English	Español	Pronunciation
cheese	*queso*	KEH-soh
American cheese	*queso americano*	KEH-soh ah-meh-ree-KAH-noh
blue cheese	*queso azul*	KEH-soh ah-SOOL
cheddar cheese	*queso cheddar*	KEH-soh CHEH-thar
cottage cheese	*requesón*	rreh-keh-SOHN
	queso blanco grumoso	KEH-soh BLAHN-koh groo-MOH-soh
cream cheese	*queso crema*	KEH-soh KREH-mah
fresh cheese	*queso fresco*	KEH-soh FREHS-koh

English	Español	Pronunciation
Monterey Jack cheese	*queso monterey jack*	KEH-soh mohn-teh-reh JAHK
mozzarella cheese	*queso mozzarella*	KEH-soh moht-seh-REH-lah
swiss cheese	*queso suizo*	KEH-soh SWEE-soh
white cheese	*queso blanco*	KEH-soh BLAHN-koh
white cheese made with cow's milk	*queso asadero*	KEH-soh ah-sah-DEH-roh
	chihuahua	chee-WAH-wah
	oaxaca	wah-HAH-kah
	queso fresco	KEH-soh FREHS-koh

Other Foods and Drinks

Spices and Herbs

English	Español	Pronunciation
spices and herbs	*especias y hierbas*	ehs-PEH-see-ahs ee YEHR-bahs
achiote (seasoning paste made from annatto seeds)	*achiote*	ah-chee-YOH-teh

English	Español	Pronunciation
chili powder (contains garlic and cumin)	*chile en polvo*	CHEE-leh ehn POHL-boh
cilantro/coriander[a]	*cilantro*	see-LAHN-troh
	cilandro	see-LAHND-roh
	culantro	koo-LAHN-troh
	coriandro	koh-ree-AHN-droh
cinnamon	*canela*	kah-NEH-lah
cumin	*comino*	koh-MEE-noh
garlic	*ajo*	AH-hoh
garlic clove	*diente de ajo*	dee-EHN-teh deh AH-hoh
garlic salt	*sal de ajo*	sahl deh AH-hoh
nutmeg	*nuez moscada*	noo-EHS mohs-KAH-thah
oregano	*orégano*	oh-REH-gah-noh
parsley	*perejil*	peh-reh-HEEL
pepper (black)	*pimienta negra*	pee-mee-YEHN-tah NEH-grah
pepper (white)	*pimienta blanca*	pee-mee-YEHN-tah BLAHN-kah

[a] Coriander can refer to the leaves (used as a herb) or the seeds (used as a spice) of the plant. Cilantro refers only to the leaves.

English	Español	Pronunciation
salt	*sal*	sahl
salt-free	*sin sal*	seen sahl
low-salt	*bajo en sal*	BAH-hoh ehn sahl
low-sodium	*bajo en sodio*	BAH-hoh ehn SOH-thee-oh
	reducido en sodio	rreh-thoo-SEE-thoh ehn SOH-thee-oh
sugar	*azúcar*	ah-SOO-kahr
sugar, dark brown, unrefined	*piloncillo*	pee-lohn-SEE-yoh
	azúcar negra	ah-SOO-kahr NEH-grah
sugar, brown or light brown	*azúcar rubia*	ah-SOO-kahr RROO-bee-yah
	azúcar morena	ah-SOO-kahr moh-REH-nah

Nuts

English	Español	Pronunciation
nuts	*nueces*	noo-EH-sehs
	frutos secos	FROO-tohs SEH-kohs
almonds	*almendras*	ahl-MEHN-drahs

Other Foods and Drinks

English	Español	Pronunciation
cashews	*anacardos*	ah-nah-KAHR-thohs
	castaña de cajú	kahs-TAHN-yah deh kah-HOO
	marañones	mah-rahn-YOH-nehs
hazelnuts	*avellanas*	ah-beh-YAHN-ahs
peanuts	*cacahuates*	kah-kah-WAH-tehs
	maníes	mah-NEE-yehs
pecans	*pacanas*	pah-KAH-nahs
	nueces	noo-EH-sehs
pine nuts	*piñones*	peen-YOH-nehs
pumpkin seeds	*pepitas*	peh-PEE-tahs
walnuts	*nueces de Castilla*	noo-EH-sehs deh kahs-TEE-yah
	nueces	noo-EH-sehs
	nueces de nogal	noo-EH-sehs deh noh-GAHL

Grains, Rice, and Flour

English	Español	Pronunciation
barley	*cebada*	seh-BAH-thah
bran	*salvado*	sahl-BAH-thoh

English	Español	Pronunciation
flour	*harina*	ah-REE-nah
wheat flour	*harina de trigo*	ah-REE-nah deh TREE-goh
whole grain flour	*harina (de trigo) integral*	ah-REE-nah (deh TREE-goh) een-teh-GRAHL
masa (corn-based dough for tamales or tortillas)	*masa*	MAH-sah
oats/oatmeal	*avena*	ah-BEH-nah
quinoa	*quínoa*	KEEN-wah
rice	*arroz*	ah-RROHS
brown rice	*arroz integral*	ah-RROHS een-teh-GRAHL
	arroz moreno	ah-RROHS moh-REH-noh
white rice	*arroz blanco*	ah-RROHS BLAHN-koh
wild rice	*arroz silvestre*	ah-RROHS seel-BEHS-treh
	arroz salvaje	ah-RROHS sahl-BAH-heh

Other Foods and Drinks

English	Español	Pronunciation
whole wheat	*de trigo integral*	deh TREE-goh een-teh-GRAHL
whole grain	*integral*	een-teh-GRAHL

Oils and Fat

English	Español	Pronunciation
butter or lard	*manteca*	mahn-TEH-kah
	grasa animal	GRAH-sah ah-nee-MAHL
	grasa de cerdo	GRAH-sah deh SEHR-doh
margarine	*margarina*	mahr-gah-REE-nah
	aceite vegetal hidrogenado	ah-SEH-ee-teh beh-heh-TAHL ee-droh-heh-NAH-thoh
oil	*aceite*	ah-SEH-ee-teh
canola oil	*aceite de canola*	ah-SEH-ee-teh deh kah-NOH-lah
corn oil	*aceite de maíz*	ah-SEH-ee-teh deh mah-EES
olive oil	*aceite de oliva*	ah-SEH-ee-teh deh oh-LEE-bah
soybean oil	*aceite de soya*	ah-SEH-ee-teh deh SOH-yah

CHAPTER 19

Counseling Terms and Phrases

Introductory Conversation
Food Preferences: What Do You Like to Eat?

In addition to knowing when (*¿cuándo?*; KWAHN-doh?) your clients eat (refer to the dialogue in Chapter 11), you need to know what they eat and—more importantly—what they like and do not like to eat. Here are some questions and phrases relating to food preferences.

English	Español	Pronunciation
What do you like to eat?	*¿Qué le gusta comer (a usted)?*	keh leh GOOS-tah koh-MEHR (ah oo-STEHD)?

English	Español	Pronunciation
I like to eat …	*Me gusta comer …*	meh-GOOS-tah koh-MEHR …
Tell me what you usually eat for breakfast, for lunch, for dinner, for snacks.	*Dígame lo que usualmente come para el desayuno, el almuerzo, la cena, y como merienda.*	DEE-gah-meh loh keh oo-soo-ahl-MEHN-teh KO-meh pah-rah ehl deh-sah-OO-noh, ehl ahl-MWEHR-soh, lah SEH-nah, ee koh-moh meh-ree-EHN-dah.
What don't you like to eat?	*¿Qué no le gusta comer (a usted)?*	keh noh leh GOOS-tah koh-MEHR (ah oo-STEHD)?
I don't like to eat …	*No me gusta comer …*	noh meh-GOOS-tah koh-MEHR …
Do you like …?	*¿Le gusta …?*	leh GOOS-tah …?
Yes, I like …	*Sí, me gusta …*	see, meh GOOS-tah …
No, I don't like …	*No, no me gusta …*	noh, noh meh GOOS-tah …
What can't you eat?	*¿Qué le hace daño?*	keh leh AH-seh DAHN-yoh?
I cannot eat dairy products.	*Me hacen daño los productos lácteos.*	meh AH-sehn DAHN-yoh lohs proh-DOOK-tohs LAHK-teh-ohs.

Counseling Terms

These questions and phrases can incorporate the Spanish words for meals and times that were provided in previous chapters. Read the following example dialogue between a nutrition professional *(nutricionista;* noo-tree-see-oh-NEES-tah) and a client *(cliente;* klee-EHN-teh):

NUTRITION PROFESSIONAL:
Señora Mendoza, what do you like to eat for breakfast?

NUTRICIONISTA:
Señora Mendoza, ¿Qué le gusta comer para el desayuno?
(sehn-YOH-rah mehn-DOH-sah, keh leh GOOS-tah koh-MEHR pah-rah ehl deh-sah-YOO-noh?)

NUTRITION PROFESSIONAL:
For breakfast I like to eat fruits.

CLIENTE:
Para el desayuno me gusta comer frutas.
(pah-rah ehl deh-sah-YOO-noh meh GOOS-tah koh-MEHR FROO-tahs.)

NUTRITION PROFESSIONAL:
What fruits do you like to eat?

NUTRICIONISTA:
¿Qué frutas le gusta comer?
(keh-FROO-tahs leh GOOS-tah koh-MEHR?)

NUTRITION PROFESSIONAL:
I like mango very much.

CLIENTE:
Me gusta mucho el mango.
(meh GOOS-tah MOO-choh ehl MAHN-goh.)

NUTRITION PROFESSIONAL:
And what don't you like to eat for breakfast?

NUTRICIONISTA:
¿Y qué no le gusta comer a usted para el desayuno?
(ee keh noh leh GOOS-tah koh-MEHR ah oo-STEHD pah-rah ehl deh-sah-YOO-noh?)

NUTRITION PROFESSIONAL:
I don't like to eat eggs.

CLIENTE:
No me gusta comer huevos.
(noh meh GOOS-tah koh-MEHR WEH-bohs.)

NUTRITION PROFESSIONAL:
I don't like to eat eggs either.

NUTRICIONISTA:
No me gusta comer huevos tampoco.
(noh meh GOOS-tah koh-MEHR WEH-bohs tahm-POH-koh.)

What Should I Eat? What Should I Drink?

When counseling your clients about their diets, the following questions and answers will be used frequently.

> *In the following examples,* beber *or* tomar *can be used interchangeably for the verb* to drink.

English	Español	Pronunciation
What should I eat?	*¿Qué debo comer?*	keh DEH-boh koh-MEHR?
You should eat ...	*Usted debiera comer ...*	oo-STEHD deh-bee-EH-rah koh-MEHR ...
What should I drink?	*¿Qué debo beber?*	keh DEH-boh beh-BEHR?
	¿Qué debo tomar?	keh DEH-boh toh-MAHR?
You should drink ...	*Usted debiera beber ...*	oo-STEHD deh-bee-EH-rah beh-BEHR ...
	Usted debiera tomar ...	oo-STEHD deh-bee-EH-rah toh-MAHR ...
What shouldn't I eat?	*¿Qué no debo comer?*	keh noh DEH-boh koh-MEHR?
You should not eat ...	*Usted no debiera comer ...*	oo-STEHD noh deh-bee-EH-rah koh-MEHR ...
What shouldn't I drink?	*¿Qué no debo beber?*	keh noh DEH-boh beh-BEHR?
	¿Qué no debo tomar?	keh noh DEH-boh toh-MAHR?
You should not drink ...	*Usted no debiera beber ...*	oo-STEHD noh deh-bee-EH-rah beh-BEHR ...
	Usted no debiera tomar ...	oo-STEHD noh deh-bee-EH-rah toh-MAHR ...

Counseling Terms

English	Español	Pronunciation
What can I eat?	¿Qué puedo comer?	keh PWEH-thoh koh-MEHR?
You can eat …	Usted puede comer …	oo-STEHD PWEH-theh koh-MEHR …
What can I drink?	¿Qué puedo beber?	keh PWEH-thoh beh-BEHR?
	¿Qué puedo tomar?	keh PWEH-thoh toh-MAHR?
You can drink …	Usted puede beber …	oo-STEHD PWEH-theh beh-BEHR …
	Usted puede tomar …	oo-STEHD PWEH-theh toh-MAHR …
What can't I eat?	¿Qué no puedo comer?	keh noh PWEH-thoh koh-MEHR?
You shouldn't eat …	Usted no debiera comer …	oo-STEHD noh deh-bee-EH-rah koh-MEHR ….
What can't I drink?	¿Qué no puedo beber?	keh noh PWEH-thoh beh-BEHR?
	¿Qué no puedo tomar?	keh noh PWEH-thoh toh-MAHR?

English	Español	Pronunciation
You shouldn't drink . . .	*Usted no debiera beber . . .*	oo-STEHD noh deh-bee-EH-rah beh-BEHR . . .
	Usted no debiera tomar . . .	oo-STEHD noh deh-bee-EH-rah toh-MAHR . . .
What do I need to eat?	*¿Qué necesito comer?*	keh neh-seh-SEE-toh koh-MEHR?
You need to eat . . .	*Usted necesita comer . . .*	oo-STEHD neh-seh-SEE-tah koh-MEHR . . .
What do I need to drink?	*¿Qué necesito beber?*	keh neh-seh-SEE-toh beh-BEHR?
	¿Qué necesito tomar?	keh neh-seh-SEE-toh toh-MAHR?
You need to drink . . .	*Usted necesita beber . . .*	oo-STEHD neh-seh-SEE-tah beh-BEHR . . .
	Usted necesita tomar . . .	oo-STEHD neh-seh-SEE-tah toh-MAHR . . .

Counseling Terms

Nutrition Guidelines

English	Español	Pronunciation
It's good to (you should) drink plenty of water every day.	*Usted debiera beber bastante agua cada día.*	oo-STEHD deh-bee-EH-rah beh-BEHR bahs-TAHN-teh AH-gwah kah-thah DEE-ah.
	Usted debiera tomar bastante agua cada día.	oo-STEHD deh-bee-EH-rah toh-MAHR bahs-TAHN-teh AH-gwah kah-thah-DEE-ah.
Vegetables are high in fiber and low in fat.	*Los vegetales son altos en[a] fibra y bajos en[b] grasa.*	lohs beh-heh-TAH-lehs sohn AHL-tohs ehn FEE-brah ee BAH-hohs ehn GRAH-sah.
It's good to (you should) eat [insert number] portions of [insert food].	*Usted debiera comer [insert number] por-ciones de [insert type of food].*	oo-STEHD deh-bee-EH-rah koh-MEHR [insert number] pohr-see-OH-nehs deh [insert type of food].
It's good to (you should) eat five fruits and vege-tables a day.	*Usted debiera comer cinco fru-tas y vegetales cada día.*	oo-STEHD deh-bee-EH-rah koh-MEHR SEEN-koh FROO-tahs ee beh-heh-TAH-lehs kah-thah DEE-ah.

---

[a] Altos en is *often pronounced as one word, AHL-toh-sehn.*
[b] Bajos en is *often pronounced as one word, BAH-hoh-sen.*

English	Español	Pronunciation
It would be good for you to eat every 3 hours.	*Usted debiera comer cada tres horas.*	oo-STEHD deh-bee-EH-rah koh-MEHR kah-thah trehs OH-rahs.

Frequently Used Words and Phrases in Counseling

Following are additional words and phrases that you will use frequently when counseling clients. Use these words and the questions and answers from the previous chapters to role-play a counseling situation.

Phrases and Terms for Use with Numbers

English	Español	Pronunciation
about or around (with time or numbers)	*más o menos*	mahs oh MEH-nohs
approximately	*aproximadamente*	ah-PROHK-see-mah-thah-MEHN-teh
every____days	*cada ____ días*	kah-thah ___ DEE-ahs
every ____ hours	*cada ____ horas*	kah-thah ___ OH-rahs

Counseling Terms

English	Español	Pronunciation
gram(s)	*gramo(s)*	GRAH-moh(s)
how many?	*¿cuántos?*	KWAHN-tohs?
	¿cuántas?	KWAHN-tahs?
percent	*porciento*	pohr-see-EHN-toh
30%	*(el) treinta porciento*	ehl TREHN-tah pohr-see-EHN-toh
percentage	*porcentaje*	pohr-sehn-TAH-heh

Energy and Macronutrients

English	Español	Pronunciation
calorie(s)	*caloría(s)*	kah-loh-REE-ah(s)
carbohydrate(s)	*carbohidrato(s)*	kahr-boh-ee-DRAH-toh(s)
sugar	*azúcar*	ah-SOO-kahr
	azúcares	ah-SOO-kah-rehs
fiber	*fibra*	FEE-brah
energy	*energía*	eh-nehr-HEE-ah
fat	*grasa*	GRAH-sah
cholesterol	*colesterol*	koh-lehs-teh-ROHL
saturated fat	*grasa saturada*	GRAH-sah sah-too-RAH-thah

English	Español	Pronunciation
unsaturated fat	*grasa no saturada*	GRAH-sah noh sah-too-RAH-thah
	grasa insaturada	GRAH-sah een-sah-too-RAH-thah
monounsaturated fat	*grasa monoinsaturada*	GRAH-sah moh-noh-een-sah-tuh-RAH-thah
polyunsaturated fat	*grasa poliinsaturada*	GRAH-sah poh-lee-een-sah-tuh-RAH-thah
protein	*proteína*	proh-teh-EE-nah

Micronutrients

English	Español	Pronunciation
folic acid	*ácido fólico*	AH-see-thoh FOH-lee-koh
iron	*hierro*	ee-EH-rroh
minerals	*minerales*	mee-neh-RAH-lehs
magnesium	*magnesio*	mahg-NEH-see-oh
phosphorus	*fósforo*	FOHS-foh-roh
potassium	*potasio*	poh-TAH-see-oh
selenium	*selenio*	seh-LEH-nee-oh
sodium	*sodio*	SOH-thee-oh
vitamin(s)	*vitamina(s)*	bee-tah-MEE-nah(s)

Dieting and Weight

English	Español	Pronunciation
diet	*dieta*	dee-EH-tah
	régimen	RREH-hee-mehn
to go on a diet	*ponerse a dieta*	poh-NEHR-seh ah dee-EH-tah
	ponerse a régimen	poh-NEHR-seh ah RREH-hee-mehn
in order to gain weight	*para subir de peso*	pah-rah soo-BEER deh PEH-soh
	para engordar	pah-rah ehn-gohr-DAHR
in order to lose weight	*para perder peso*	pah-rah pehr-DEHR PEH-soh
	para bajar de peso	pah-rah bah-HAHR deh PEH-soh
	para adelgazar	pah-rah ah-dehl-gah-SAHR

Other Phrases and Terms

English	Español	Pronunciation
Does it have…?	*¿Tiene…?*	tee-EH-neh?
It has…	*Tiene…*	tee-EH-neh

English	Español	Pronunciation
excessive intake	*consumo excesivo*	kohn-SOO-moh ehk-seh-SEE-boh
healthy	*sano*	SAH-noh
	saludable	sah-loo-DAH-bleh
good for the health	*bueno/a[a] para la salud*	BWEH-noh/nah[a] pah-rah lah sah-LOOD
bad for the health	*malo/a[a] para la salud*	MAH-loh/lah[a] pah-rah lah sah-LOOD
high in . . .	*alto/a[a] en . . .* *rico/a[a] en . . .*	AHL-toh/tah[a] ehn RREE-koh/kah[a] ehn
label	*etiqueta*	eh-tee-KEH-tah
low in . . .	*bajo/a[a] en . . .*	BAH-hoh/hah[a] ehn
(in) moderation	*(con) moderación*	(kohn) moh-deh-rah-see-OHN
nutritious	*nutritivo/a[a]*	noo-tree-tee-boh/bah[a]
servings size/ portions	*raciones* *porciónes*	rrah-see-OH-nehs pohr-see-OH-nehs
too much	*demasiado/a[a]*	deh-mah-see-AH-thoh/thah[a]
	excesivo/a[a]	ehk-seh-SEE-boh/bah[a]

[a]   *These adjectives can end in either the letter "o" or "a," depending on the gender of the noun that the adjective modifies. See Chapter 7 for more on this topic.*

Questions the Client May Ask

English	Español	Pronunciation
How many calories does [insert food] have?	¿Cuántas calorías tiene [insert food]?	KWAHN-tahs kah-loh-REE-ahs tee-EH-neh [insert food name]?
[Insert food] has [insert number] calories.	[Insert food] tiene [insert number] calorías.	[Insert food name] tee-EH-neh [insert number] kah-loh-REE-ahs.
Should I lose weight?	¿Debo perder peso?	DEH-boh pehr-dehr PEH-soh?
	¿Debo bajar de peso?	DEH-boh bah-HAHR deh PEH-soh?

Additional Diet History Questions

Here are some questions you may need to ask a client, along with some possible answers.

Age

English	Español	Pronunciation
How old are you?	¿Cuántos años tiene usted?	KWAHN-tohs AHN-yohs tee-EH-neh oo-STEHD?
	¿Qué edad tiene usted?	keh eh DAD tee–EH-neh oo-STEHD?
I'm _____ years old.	Tengo _____ años.	tehn-goh _____ AHN-yohs.

Height, Weight, and Exercise

English	Español	Pronunciation
How tall are you?	¿Qué altura tiene?	keh ahl-TOO-rah tee-EH-neh?
What do you usually weigh?	¿Cuánto pesa usted normalmente?	KWAHN-toh PEH-sah oo-STEHD nohr-mahl-MEHN-teh?
I weigh _____ pounds.	Peso _____ libras.	PEH-soh _____ LEE-brahs
Have you gained or lost 5 pounds in the last few months?	¿Ha subido o perdido 5 libras en los últimos pocos meses?	ah soo-BEE-thoh oh pehr-dee-thoh SEEN-koh LEE-brahs ehn lohs OOL-tee-mohs poh-kohs MEH-sehs?

English	Español	Pronunciation
How much weight have you gained?	*¿Cuánto peso ha aumentado?*	KWAHN-toh PEH-soh ah ow-mehn-TAH-thoh?
What was your prepregnancy weight?	*¿Cuánto pesaba usted antes de quedar embarazada?*	KWAHN-toh peh-SAH-bah oo-STEHD AHN-tehs deh keh-THAHR ehm-bah-rah-SAH-thah?
Do you exercise?	*¿Hace usted ejercicio?*	AH-seh oo-STEHD eh-hehr-SEE-see-oh?
If so, what type and how often?	*Si es que sí, ¿de qué tipo y con qué frecuencia?*	see ehs keh see, deh keh TEE-poh ee kohn keh freh-KWEHN-see-ah?
For how long?	*¿Por cuánto tiempo?*	pohr KWAHN-toh tee-EHM-poh?

Shopping, Cooking, and Eating Out

English	Español	Pronunciation
Who buys the food you eat?	¿Quién compra la comida que come?	kee-EHN KOHM-prah lah koh-MEE-thah keh KOH-meh?
Do you cook?	¿Usted cocina?	oo-STEHD koh-SEE-nah?
How often do you eat in a restaurant?	¿Con qué frecuencia come en un restaurante?	kohn keh-freh-KWEHN-see-ah KOH-meh en oon reh-stow-RAHN-teh?

Cultural Tidbit

Most Spanish-speaking countries use the metric system and measure body weight in kilograms (*kilos*; KEE-lohs). If the answer to the question, "How much do you weigh?" seems very low, the client is probably giving his or her weight in kilograms. The conversions for units of weight are:

Weight in pounds / 2.2 = Weight in kilograms

Weight in kilograms × 2.2 = Weight in pounds

Dairy Intake

English	Español	Pronunciation
Do you drink milk?	*¿Bebe usted leche?*	BEH-beh oo-STEHD LEH-cheh?
	¿Toma usted leche?	TOH-mah oo-STEHD LEH-cheh?
What kind?	*¿Qué clase?*	keh KLAH-seh?
	¿Qué tipo?	keh TEE-poh?
	¿De cuál?	deh KWAHL?
Are you lactose intolerant?	*¿Tiene usted intolerancia a la lactosa?*	tee-EH-neh oo-STEHD een-toh-leh-RAHN-see-ah ah lah lahk-TOH-sah?
With what symptoms?	*¿Qué sintomas le da?*	keh SEEN-toh-mahs leh dah?

Family History

English	Español	Pronunciation
Does diabetes run in your family?	*¿Tiene familiares con diabetes?*	tee-EH-neh fah-mee-lee-AH-rehs kohn dee-ah-BEH-tehs?
Does heart disease run in your family?	*¿Tiene familiares con enfermedades del corazón?*	tee-EH-neh fah-mee-lee-AH-rehs kohn ehn-fehr-meh-DAH-thehs dehl koh-rah-SOHN?

Medical History

English	Español	Pronunciation
Do you have problems with your stomach? (heartburn, acid reflux)	*¿Tiene problemas con el estómago? (acidez, reflujo esofágico)*	tee-EH-neh proh-BLEH-mahs kohn ehl eh-STOH-mah-goh? (ah-see-THEHS, rreh-FLOO-hoh eh-soh-FAH-hee-koh)
Has anyone ever talked to you about a special diet?	*¿Alguna vez alguien le ha sugerido una dieta especial?*	ahl-GOON-ah behs AHL-gee-ehn leh ah soo-heh-REE-thoh OO-nah dee-EH-tah eh-speh-see-ahl?
Have you ever had surgery?	*¿Le han operado alguna vez?*	leh ahn oh-peh-RAH-thoh ahl-goon-ah BEHS?
If so, what for?	*¿Si es así,[a] qué tipo de operación?*	see ehs ah-SEE, keh TEE-poh theh oh-peh-rah-see-OHN?
Have you been diagnosed with heart disease, diabetes, hypertension, cancer, or other health problems?	*¿Le han diagnosticado con enfermedad del corazón, diabetes, hipertensión, cáncer, u otros problemas de la salud?*	leh ahn dee-ahg-noh-stee-KAH-thoh kohn ehn-fehr-meh-THAD dehl koh-rah-SOHN, dee-ah-BEH-tehs, ee-pehr-tehn-see-OHN, KAHN-sehr, oo OH-trohs proh-BLEH-mahs deh lah sah-LOOD?

[a] Es así is *often pronounced as one word, eh-sah-SEE.*

English	Español	Pronunciation
If so, what was the health problem?	¿Si es así,[a] cuál fue el problema de salud?	see ehs ah-SEE, KWAHL fweh ehl proh-BLEH-mah deh sah-LOOD?
Have you seen a healer or other nonmedical person for your condition?	¿Ha visto un curandero u otra persona que no es médico para su condición?	ah VEES-toh uhn cuh-rahn-DEH-roh oo OH-trah pehr-SOH-nah keh noh ehs MEH-dee-koh PAH-rah soo kohn-dee-see-OHN?
What did this person recommend?	¿Qué le recomendó esa persona?	keh leh reh-koh-mehn-DOH EH-sah pehr-SOH-nah?
Are you using that treatment?	¿Está usando ese tratamiento?	eh-STAH oo-SAHN-doh EH-seh trah-tah-mee-EHN-toh?

[a] Es así is often pronounced as one word, eh-sah-SEE.

Medication Use

English	Español	Pronunciation
Do you take any medications?	¿Toma usted medicamentos?	TOH-mah oo-STEHD meh-dee-kah-MEHN-tohs?
	¿Toma usted alguna medicación?	TOH-mah oo-STEHD ahl-GOON-ah meh-thee-kah-see-OHN?

English	Español	Pronunciation
Yes, I take …	*Sí, tomo …*	see, TOH-moh …
What herbs or diet supplements do you take now?	*¿Toma usted algún suplemento dietético o té de hierbas?*	TOH-mah oo-STEHD ahl-GOON soo-pleh-MEHN-toh dee-eh-TEH-tee-koh oh teh theh yee-EHR-bahs?
What/which do you take?	*¿Cuál toma (usted)?*	kwahl TOH-mah oo-STEHD?

Alcohol Intake and Smoking

English	Español	Pronunciation
Do you drink alcohol?	*¿Toma alcohol?*	TOH-mah ahl-KOHL?
How many alcoholic drinks do you have per day?	*¿Cuántas bebidas alcohólicas toma al día?*	KWAHN-tahs beh-BEE-thahs ahl-KOH-lee-kahs TOH-mah ahl DEE-ah?
How many alcoholic drinks do you have per week?	*¿Cuántas bebidas alcohólicas toma a la semana?*	KWAHN-tahs beh-BEE-thahs ahl-KOH-lee-kahs TOH-mah ah lah seh-MAH-nah?
Do you smoke? If so, how often?	*¿Fuma? ¿Si es así,[a] con qué frecuencia?*	FOO-mah? see ehs-ah-SEE, kohn keh freh-KWEHN-see-ah?

[a] Es así *is often pronounced as one word,* eh-sah-SEE.

Diseases and Conditions

You can use the following vocabulary to discuss diseases or conditions your client may have.

Diseases and Disorders

English	Español	Pronunciation
Do you have…?	¿Tiene usted…?	tee-EH-neh oo-STEHD…?
I have…	Tengo…	TEHN-goh…
(a) disease	(una) enfermedad	(OO-nah) ehn-fehr-meh-DAHD
(a) disorder	(un) trastorno	(OON) trahs-TOHR-noh
anemia	anemia	ah-NEH-mee-ah
anorexia (nervosa)	anorexia (nerviosa)	ah-noh-REK-see-ah (nehr-bee-OH sah)
bulimia (nervosa)	bulimia (nerviosa)	boo-LEE-mee-ah (nehr-bee-OH-sah)
blood	sangre	SAHN-greh
difficulty swallowing	problemas al tragar	proh-BLEH-mahs ahl trah-GAHR
difficulty chewing	problemas al masticar	proh-BLEH-mahs ahl mahs-tee-KAHR

English	Español	Pronunciation
headaches	*dolores de cabeza*	doh-LOH-rehs deh kah-BEH-sah
hunger	*hambre*	AHM-breh
thirst	*sed*	sehd
malnutrition	*desnutrición*	dehs-noo-tree-see-OHN
heartburn/ acid reflux	*acidéz/ reflujo ácido*	ah-see-THEHS/ rreh-FLOO-hoh AH-see-thoh
gas/ flatulence	*gases/ flatulencia*	GAH-sehs/ flah-too-LEHN-see-ah
indigestion	*indigestión*	een-dee-heh-stee-OHN
bowel movement/ feces	*excremento*	eks-kreh-MEHN-toh
	popo; caca (informal)	POH-poh; KAH-kah
loose stools	*excrementos sueltos*	ehk-skreh-MEHN-tohs SWEHL-tohs
	heces sueltas	EH-sehs SWEHL-tahs
constipation	*estreñimiento*	ehs-trehn-yee-mee-EHN-toh
	constipación	kohn-stee-pah-see-OHN
	sequedad de vientre	seh-keh-THAD deh bee-EHN-treh

English	Español	Pronunciation
diarrhea	*diarrea*	dee-ah-RREH-ah
urine	*orina*	oh-REE-nah
	pipi; chi (informal)	PEE-pee; chee
gluten allergy	*alergia al gluten*	ah-LEHR-hee-ah ahl GLOO-tehn
lactose intolerance	*intolerancia a la lactosa*	een-toh-leh-RAHN-see-ah ah lah lahk-TOH-sah
high blood pressure	*presión (arterial) alta*	preh-see-OHN (ahr-teh-ree-AHL) AHL-tah
	alta presión	AHL-tah preh-see-OHN
low blood pressure	*presión (arterial) baja*	preh-see-OHN (ahr-teh-ree-AHL) BAH-hah
	baja presión	BAH-hah preh-see-OHN
high cholesterol	*colesterol alto*	koh-lehs-teh-ROHL AHL-toh
nausea	*nauseas*	NOW-see-ahs
vomit	*vómito(s)*	BOH-mee-toh(s)
liver disease	*enfermedad del hígado*	ehn-fehr-meh-DAHD dehl EE-gah-thoh

English	Español	Pronunciation
renal disease	*enfermedad renal*	ehn-fehr-meh-DAHD rreh-NAHL
	enfermedad de los riñones	ehn-fehr-meh-DAHD deh lohs rreen-YOH-nehs
obesity	*obesidad*	oh-beh-see-DAHD
	gordura	gohr-DOO-rah
overweight	*sobrepeso*	soh-breh-PEH-soh

Diabetes

English	Español	Pronunciation
Do you have …?	*¿Tiene usted …?*	tee-EH-neh oo-STEHD?
Do you do…?	*¿Hace usted …?*	AH-seh oo-STEHD?
Do you check …?	*¿Revisa usted…?*	rreh-BEE-sah oo-STEHD?
Foods that contain carbohydrates are…	*Comidas que contienen carbohidratos son…*	ko-MEE-thahs keh kohn-tee-EH-nehn kahr-boh-ee-DRAH-tohs sohn…
blood sugar goal	*meta para azúcar en la sangre*	MEH-tah pah-rah ah-SOO-kahr ehn lah SAHN-greh
blurry vision	*vista borrosa*	BEES-tah boh-RROH-sah

English	Español	Pronunciation
dairy (like milk, yogurt)	*productos lácteos (como leche, yogur)*	proh-DOOK-tohs LAHK-teh-ohs (KOH-moh LEH-cheh, yoh-GUHR)
desserts and sweets (like *churro, buñuelo,* candy, cake, sugar-sweetened soda)	*postres y dulces (como churro, buñuelo, caramelos, pastel, refresco con azúcar)*	POHS-trehs ee DUHL-sehs (KOH-moh CHOO-rroh, boon-YWEH-loh, kah-rah-MEH-lohs, pah-STEHL, rreh-FREHS-koh kohn ah-SOO-kahr)
diabetes	*diabetes*	dee-ah-BEH-tehs
gestational diabetes	*diabetes gestacional*	dee-ah-BEH-tehs hehs-tah-see-oh-NAHL
	diabetes del embarazo	dee-ah-BEH-tehs dehl ehm-bah-RAH-soh
grains (like tortillas, bread, and cereal)	*granos (como tortillas, pan y cereales)*	GRAH-nohs (KOH-moh tohr-TEE-yahs, pahn, ee seh-reh-AH-lehs)
fat	*grasa*	GRAH-sah
feet/foot	*pie/pies*	pee-EH/pee-EHS
fiber	*fibra*	FEE-brah

English	Español	Pronunciation
finger stick	*determinación de glucemia capilar*	deh-tehr-mee-nah-see-YOHN theh gloo-CEH-mee-ah kah-pee-LAHR
	medir el azúcar en la sangre picando un dedo	meh-DIHR ehl ah-SOO-kahr ehn lah SAHN-greh pee-KAHN-doh on DEH-thoh
fruits (including juices)	*frutas (incluyendo jugos)*	FRUH-tahs (een-kluh-YEHN-doh-HOO-gohs)
hyperglycemia	*hiperglucemia*	ee-pehr-gloo-SEH-mee-yah
hypoglycemia	*hipoglucemia*	ee-poh-gloo-SEH-mee-yah
lancet	*lanceta*	lahn-SEH-tah
legumes (beans)	*legumbres (frijoles)*	leh-GOOM-brehs (free-HOH-lehs)
portion/ serving size	*porción*	pohr-see-OHN
pancreas	*páncreas*	PAHN-kreh-ahs
protein	*proteína*	proh-teh-EEN-ah
sugar	*azúcar*	ah-SOO-kahr

English	Español	Pronunciation
starchy vegetables (like corn or potatoes)	verduras ricas en almidón (como maíz o papas)	behr-DOO-rahs RREE-kahs ehn ahl-mee-DOHN (KOH-moh mah-EES oh PAH-pahs)
test strip	tira de ensayo	TEE-rah deh ehn-SAH-yoh
thirst	sed	sehd
tired/lack of energy	sueño/falta de energía	SWEHN-yoh/FAHL-tah theh eh-nehr-HEE-ah
units of insulin	unidades de insulina	oo-nee-DAH-thehs deh een-soo-LEE-nah
Which of the carbohydrate foods are most important to you?	¿Cuáles de las comidas que contienen carbohidratos le importan más?	KWAH-lehs deh lahs koh-MEE-thahs keh kohn-tee-EH-nehn kahr-boh-ee-DRAH-tohs leh eem-POHR-tahn MAHS?

Food Allergies

English	Español	Pronunciation
Do you have any food allergies?	¿Le hace daño algún alimento?	leh ah-seh DAHN-yoh ahl-GOON ah-lee-MEHN-toh?
	¿Tiene (usted) alergia a algún alimento?	tee-EHN-neh oo-STEHD ah-LEHR-hee-ya ah ahl-GOON ah-lee-MEHN-toh?

Counseling Terms

Eating Disorders

English	Español	Pronunciation
Are you . . . ?	¿Es usted . . . ?	ehs oo-STEHD . . . ?
I am . . .	Soy . . .	Soy . . .
anorexic	anoréxico/a[a]	ah-noh-REK-see-koh/kah[a]
bulimic	bulímico/a[a]	boo-LEE-mee-koh/kah[a]

[a] These adjectives can end in either the letter "o" or "a," depending on the gender of the person with the condition. See Chapter 7 for more on this topic.

Pregnancy and Lactation

English	Español	Pronunciation
Are you pregnant?	¿Está usted embarazada?	ehs-TAH oo-STEHD ehm-bah-rah-SAH-thah?
I am pregnant.	Estoy embarazada.	ehs-TOY ehm-bah-rah-SAH-thah
When are you due to deliver?	¿Cuándo va a dar a luz?	KWAHN-doh bah ah dahr ah LOOS?
	¿Cuándo va a aliviarse?	KWAHN-doh bah ah ah-lee-bee-AHR-seh?
Are you breastfeeding?	¿Está usted amamantando?	ehs-TAH oo-STEHD ah-mah-mahn-TAHN-doh?
	¿Está usted dando el pecho?	ehs-TAH oo-STEHD DAHN-doh ehl PEH-choh?

Counseling Terms

English	Español	Pronunciation
Yes, I am breastfeeding.	*Sí, estoy amamantando.*	see, ehs-TOY ah-mah-mahn-TAHN-doh.
	Sí, estoy dando el pecho.	see, ehs-TOY DAHN-doh ehl PEH-choh.
No, I am not breastfeeding.	*No, no estoy amamantando.*	noh, noh ehs-TOY ah-mah-mahn-TAHN-doh.
	No, no estoy dando el pecho.	noh, noh ehs-TOY DAHN-doh ehl PEH-choh.
latch on	*prenderse*	prehn-DEHR-seh
breast pump	*sacaleche*	sah-kah-LEH-cheh
	extractor de leche materna	ehk-strahk-TOHR deh LEH-cheh mah-TEHR-nah
colostrum	*calostro*	cah-LOH-stroh

CHAPTER 20

Cooking and Recipe Terms

Methods of Preparation

The following list contains cooking and recipe terms, which can be useful in discussing food preparation with your client.

English	Español	Pronunciation
baked	*al horno*	ahl OHR-noh
	horneado/a[a]	ohr-neh-AH-thoh/ah[a]
barbecued meat	*al carbón*	ahl kahr-BOHN

[a] These adjectives can end in either the letter "o" or "a," depending on the gender of the noun that the adjective modifies. See Chapter 7 for more on this topic.

English	Español	Pronunciation
blanch	*blanquear*	blahn-keh-AHR
	escaldar	ehs-kahl-DAHR
boiled	*hervido/a*[a]	ehr-BEE-thoh/thah[a]
braise	*estofar*	eh-stoh-FAHR
broiled	*a la parrilla*	ah lah pah-RREE-yah
brush (pan with oil)	*pincelar (asadera con aceite)*	peen-seh-LAHR (ah-sah-THEH-rah kohn ah-see-EH-teh)
	untar aceite al molde de hornear	uhn-TAHR ah-SEH-ee-teh ahl MOHL-deh deh ohr-neh-AHR
canned	*en lata*	ehn LAH-tah
	enlatado/a[a]	ehn-lah-TAH-thoh/ah[a]
chopped	*picado/a*[a]	pee-KAH-thoh/thah[a]
	troceado/a[a]	troh-seh-AH-thoh/thah[a]
cold	*frío/a*[a]	free-oh/ah[a]
cooked	*cocido/a*[a]	koh-SEE-thoh/thah[a]
cut up (*adjective*)	*cortado/a*[a]	kohr-TAH-thoh/thah[a]
debone	*deshuesar*	dehs-weh-SAHR

---

[a] *These adjectives can end in either the letter "o" or "a," depending on the gender of the noun that the adjective modifies. See Chapter 7 for more on this topic.*

English	Español	Pronunciation
dry	*seco*	SEH-koh
fat-free	*sin grasa*	seen GRAH-sah
fresh	*fresco/a*[a]	FREHS-koh/kah[a]
fried	*frito/a*[a]	FREE-toh/tah[a]
not breaded	*no empanizado/a*[a]	noh ehm-pah-nee-SAH-thoh/thah[a]
not fried	*no frito/a*[a]	noh FREE-toh/tah[a]
frozen	*congelado/a*[a]	kohn-heh-LAH-thoh/thah[a]
grate	*rallar*	rrah-YAHR
grilled	*asado/a*[a]	ah-SAH-thoh/thah[a]
hot (temperature)	*caliente*	kah-lee-EHN-teh
low-fat	*bajo/a*[a] *en grasa*	BAH-hoh/hah[a] ehn GRAH-sah
main dish	*plato principal*	PLAH-toh preen-see-PAHL
melt	*derretir*	deh-rreh-TEER
microwaved	*cocido/a*[a] *en microondas*	koh-SEE-thoh/thah[a] ehn mee-kroh-OHN dahs
mix	*mezclar*	mehs-KLAHR

[a] *These adjectives can end in either the letter "o" or "a," depending on the gender of the noun that the adjective modifies. See Chapter 7 for more on this topic.*

English	Español	Pronunciation
peel (off)	*pelar*	peh-LAHR
pickled	*en vinagre*	ehn vee-NAH-greh
prepared	*preparado/a*[a]	preh-pah-RAH-thoh/thah[a]
raw	*crudo/a*[a]	KROO-thoh/thah[a]
rinse (off)	*enjuagar*	ehn-hwah-GAHR
rolled	*enrollado*[a]	ehn-roh-YAH-thoh/thah[a]
salt-free	*sin sal*	seen sahl
with less salt	*con menos sal*	kohn MEH-nohs sahl
sautéed	*sofrito/a*[a]	soh-FREE-toh/thah[a]
	salteado/a[a]	sahl-teh-AH-thoh/thah[a]
served	*servido/a*[a]	sehr-BEE-thoh/thah[a]
skim	*descremado/a*[a]	dehs-kreh-MAH-thoh/thah[a]
(a) slice	*una rebanada*	OO-nah rreh-bah-NAH-thah
	una rodaja	OO-nah rroh-DAH-hah
	una feta	OO-nah FEH-tah

[a] *These adjectives can end in either the letter "o" or "a," depending on the gender of the noun that the adjective modifies. See Chapter 7 for more on this topic.*

English	Español	Pronunciation
sliced	*rebanado/a*[a]	rreh-bah-NAH-thoh/thah[a]
	tajado/a[a]	tah-HAH-thoh/thah[a]
spread	*untado/a*[a]	oon-TAH-thoh/thah[a]
steamed	*cocido/a*[a] *al vapor*	koh-SEE-thoh/thah[a] ahl bah-POHR
	al vapor	ahl bah-POHR
stewed[b]	*guisado/a*[a]	ghee-SAH-thoh/tah[a]
stir-fried	*sofrito/a*[a]	soh-FREE-toh/tah[a]
	salteado/a[a]	sahl-teh-AH-thoh/thah[a]
strain	*escurrir*	ehs-koo-RREER
stuffed	*relleno/a*[a]	rreh-YEH-noh/nah[a]
sugar-free	*sin azúcar*	seen ah-SOO-kahr
well-done	*bien hecho/a*[a]	bee-ehn EH-choh/chah[a]
	bien cocido/a[a]	bee-ehn koh-SEE-thoh/thah[a]
with	*con*	kohn
without	*sin*	seen

[a] *These adjectives can end in either the letter "o" or "a," depending on the gender of the noun that the adjective modifies. See Chapter 7 for more on this topic.*
[b] *This preparation uses a large amount of oil.*

Portion and Measurement Terms

English	Español	Pronunciación
clove (of garlic)	*diente (de ajo)*	dee-EHN-teh (deh AH-hoh)
cube(s)	*cubo(s)*	KOO-boh(s)
	cubitos	koo-BEE-tohs
cup(s)	*taza(s)*	TAH-sah(s)
	tazas de medir	TAH-sahs deh meh-DEER
half	*media*	MEH-thee-ah
	mitad	mee-TAHD
less	*menos*	MEH-nohs
more	*más*	mahs
ounce(s)	*onza(s)*	OHN-sah(s)
piece(s)	*trozo(s)*	TROH-soh(s)
	pedazo(s)	peh-THAH-soh(s)
small piece(s)	*trocito(s)*	troh-SEE-toh(s)
	pedacito(s)	peh-thah-SEE-toh(s)
strip(s)	*tira(s)*	TEE-rah(s)

English	Español	Pronunciation
tablespoon	*cucharada*	koo-chah-RAH-thah
teaspoon	*cucharadita*	koo-chah-rah-THEE-tah
	cucharadita tipo de té	koo-chah-rah-TEEH-tah tee-poh theh TEH

Section III

Nutrition Care Education and Resources

CHAPTER 21

Nutrition Education and the Non-English-Speaking Client

Health Literacy and Nutrition Education

According to the health literacy component of the US government's 2003 National Assessment of Adult Literacy, over one-third of US adults—77 million people—would have difficulty with common health tasks, such as following directions on a prescription drug label. All racial/ethnic groups contain adults at below-basic or basic levels of health literacy, but Hispanics have the largest percent of adults at these levels (65%). Adults ages 65 or older were more likely to have below-basic or basic health literacy than those younger than 65, and 11 million people are not literate in English.[1]

Although a 6th-grade reading level is average in the United States, most health information materials (including those for nutrition education) are written for individuals reading above the 10th-grade level. In addition, educators, including nutrition professionals, tend to overestimate their users' abilities and underestimate the complexity of the materials they provide.[2]

Health literacy is defined as the ability to obtain, process, and understand basic health information and services so that appropriate health decisions can be made. The 2003 national adult literacy data demonstrated that health information is too difficult for average Americans to use to make health decisions, and this has influenced many groups (American Medical Association, Institute of Medicine, the Joint Commission, and others) as well as the US government (ie, National Action Plan to Improve Health Literacy, 2010) to address health literacy.[1,3,4] Communicating complex nutrition and health information can be even more challenging when the nutrition professional and the client do not speak the same language. In addition, those who are able to communicate socially in English often do not have the language skills to understand nutrition and health issues.[5]

Additional Resources

If you use materials that your client cannot easily read, your message may not be understood, causing the client to feel distrust or anger. Your client may not be able to take the actions you recommend and thus may not see the value of nutrition counseling.[2] In addition, education material that is not appropriate for clients' reading level may place you out of compliance with Joint Commission National Patient Safety Goals, especially goal 13, which holds institutions accountable for providing culturally appropriate information that is understandable to clients.[3] The federal government (Plain Writing Act, 2010) has revised an earlier mandate to use "plain language."[6]

Stress, illness, pain, and some medications reduce the ability to read, learn, and remember, and many well-educated people have difficulty with health and nutrition terms and concepts.[7] Coping skills that allow a poor reader to function at work may not be useful in the face of an urgent health problem. One study estimated that low health literacy costs health care systems between $106 billion to $238 billion annually.[8]

Designing, Selecting, or Adapting Easy-to-Read Materials

You may have difficulty finding easy-to-read, culturally appropriate materials for your Latino clients.[9] Some materials may contain useful information but may not be written in an easily read format.[10] You may find that you need to design or adapt materials and resources.

Most educational materials contain too much information. Giving copious information to clients with the hope that at least some of it will be retained has the opposite effect—the more information given, the less the client remembers. Concentrating on just the key (essential) messages enhances retention and learning.[7,11]

Designing easy-to-read material is more complicated than simply writing for a low reading level. A brief overview of the attributes of easy-to-read material follows. See the resource list in Chapter 22 for further information.

Creating Content

Here are suggestions for creating content for easy-to-read educational materials:

- Limit content to three to five key messages. Adults have difficulty remembering more than five new items. Focus on need-to-know, rather than nice-to-know, directives because information overload does not enhance learning.[2,7]

- Choose simple words, like those in the list on the next page.

- Make sure the content of the material is appropriate for the client's age and culture.[2,7]

Additional Resources

Instead of ...	Try ...
absence of	no, none
accomplish	do
accurate	right
acquire	get
additional	more
alternative	choice
approximately	about
attempt	try
benefit	help
consider	think about
consult	ask, check with, talk to
contains	has
correct	right
currently	now
deficiency	lack
discontinue	stop, end, quit
disturbance	problem, change
effect	make

Instead of ...	Try ...
encourage	ask to, help
ensure	make sure
exceed	go beyond, pass
explain	tell, show
factor	cause
feasible	can be done, will work
finalize	finish up, end
for further instructions	find out what to do next
function	work, do
guidelines	steps to follow, directions
identify	show, name, find
implement	do, follow
information	facts
large numbers of	many, most
maintain	keep, look after, save
modify	change
monitor	check on, watch
notify	call, tell, let us know

Instead of . . .	Try . . .
objective	aim, goal, what we hope to do
purchase	buy
recommend	suggest, guide
requirement	need
restriction	limit
select	choose
supply	give
urgent	cannot wait long
utilize	use

Writing Text

Tips for writing successful educational materials include the following:[2,7,10,11,12,13]

- Use one of the many available resources to ensure that the information is provided at a sixth-grade reading level or below as appropriate. (See the resource list in Chapter 22.)

- Choose one- or two-syllable words whenever possible (eg, *show* instead of *demonstrate*).

- Use short sentences. A sentence should contain no more than 10 to 15 words.

- Use strong, direct language; do not use passive voice. For example, use "Your dietitian will weigh you," instead of "You will be weighed by the dietitian." (Note that a culturally sensitive translation may change some language patterns.)

- Be careful not to turn verbs into nouns. For example, choose *predicted* instead of *made the prediction*.

- Do not include unnecessary words or phrases. For example, use "This supplement may upset your stomach," instead of "This supplement may cause you to experience nausea."

- Keep the information personal. For example, use "Take your vitamins when you eat a meal."

- Give specific examples instead of abstract ideas. For example, use "Read the label. Make sure your cereal has at least 6 grams of fiber in a half-cup serving," instead of "Choose a high-fiber cereal."

- Paragraphs should be short with only a single key message in each.

Incorporating Type/Fonts

Although purists will differentiate between type and fonts, the terms are now used interchangeably rather than using font to indicate the size/style of type.[14] Some typefaces are easier to read than others. Here is some guidance for working with type and fonts[2,7,10,11]:

- Select an easily readable type, such as Garamond, Bembo, or Times. Do not incorporate more than two or three type styles on a page.

- Use uppercase and lowercase text. Many poor readers recognize words by sight, and words set in all uppercase letters may run together and look the same.

- Use at least a 12-point font size with a serif typeface.

Layout and Design

Good design helps the reader. Consider the following techniques when designing educational documents[2,7,11,15]:

- Make sure the margins are wide and include white space. Avoid using too much text. Do not clutter the page(s).

- Separate blocks of text with headings and subheadings.

- Use bulleted lists when possible.

- Choose a two-column layout.

- Justify the text on the left, but not the right. Uneven spacing between words can make reading difficult for your client.

- Choose black or dark blue ink on white or cream-colored paper. This combination (contrast) makes reading easy.

- Incorporate illustrations when they are useful additions to the content. Also, keep in mind that images of individuals should represent the culture of your intended audience.

Tips for Creating or Selecting Culturally Appropriate Materials

To be effective, educational materials must suit the audience. Consider the following when creating or selecting materials for Latino clients:

- Materials should include words Latino clients know.[2] Provide the key words in English as well so clients can begin to learn about foods in the United States.

- Your recommendations should be consistent with your client's lifestyle. For example, discuss salsa rather than another condiment.[10]

- Field-test materials with Latino clients. Listen to what they say because they will be the best judges of what is useful and appropriate. If possible, solicit opinions individually or in focus groups to improve your materials.[2,13]

- When materials are translated, ensure that the text is as simple and easy to follow as possible. Your translator should understand basic nutrition terms and concepts. Incorporate suggestions that will make the translated material easy to read. Ask that the material be translated back into English to ensure that the translation remains accurate.[7,9]

- If your intended audience consists of more than one Latino group, be certain to incorporate alternate words wherever possible. For example, depending on their country of origin, clients may use *los guisantes, los chicharos,* or *petit pois* for peas.

- Audio recordings, videos, and DVDs can be useful for clients who are poor readers or have other difficulties.[9,13]

References

1. US Department of Health and Human Services. America's health literacy: why we need accessible health information. Office of Disease Prevention and Health Promotion Health Communication Activities. 2008. https://health.gov /communication/literacy/issuebrief. Accessed June 25, 2017.

2. Root J, Stableford S. *Write It Easy-to-Read: A Guide to Creating Plain English Materials.* Biddeford, ME: University of New England; 1998.

3. The Joint Commission. *"What Did the Doctor Say?": Improving Health Literacy to Protect Patient Safety.* Oakbrook Terrace, IL: The Joint Commission; 2007. www.jointcommission.org /assets/1/18/improving_health_literacy.pdf. Accessed June 25, 2017.

4. US Department of Health and Human Services. *National Action Plan to Improve Health Literacy.* Office of Disease Prevention and Health Promotion. Washington, DC: US Department of Health and Human Services; 2010. https://health.gov/communication/HLActionPlan/pdf /Health_Literacy_Action_Plan.pdf. Accessed June 26, 2017.

5. Osborne H. *Overcoming Communication Barriers in Patient Education.* Gaithersburg, MD: Aspen Publishers; 2001.

6. Plain Language Action and Information Network. Federal plain language guidelines. Revision 1, May 2011. www.plainlanguage.gov/howto/guidelines/FederalPL Guidelines/FederalPLGuidelines.pdf. Accessed June 25, 2017.

7. Doak C, Doak L, Root J. *Teaching Patients with Low Literacy Skills.* 2nd ed. Philadelphia, PA: JB Lippincott; 1996.

8. Vernon JA, Trujillo A, Rosenbaum S, DeBuono B. *Low Health Literacy: Implications for National Health Policy.* https://publichealth.gwu.edu/departments/healthpolicy /CHPR/downloads/LowHealthLiteracyReport10_4_07.pdf. Accessed June 24, 2017.

9. Curry K, Jaffe A. *Nutrition Counseling and Communication Skills.* Philadelphia, PA: WB Saunders; 1998.

10. AMC Cancer Research Center, Center for Disease Control and Prevention. *Beyond the Brochure: Alternative Approaches to Effective Health Communication.* Denver, CO: AMC Cancer Research Center; 1994.

11. Seubert D. A tale of two handouts: applying health literacy principles to improve readability of printed patient education materials. www.healthcommunications.org/resources /handouts.pdf. Accessed June 21, 2017.

12.   Plain Language Action and Information Network.
      Simple words and phrases. www.plainlanguage.gov
      /howto/wordsuggestions/simplewords.cfm. Accessed
      June 25, 2017.

13.   Centers for Medicare and Medicaid Services. Tools for
      making written material clear and effective. www.cms.gov
      /Outreach-and-Education/Outreach/WrittenMaterials
      Toolkit/index.html?redirect=/WrittenMaterialsToolkit.
      Accessed June 19, 2017.

14.   *AIGA*. Fonts vs. typeface, explained by a designer. October 21,
      2002. www.aiga.org/theyre-not-fonts. Accessed July 26, 2017.

15.   Center for Medicare Education. Writing easy to read mate-
      rials. Issue Brief vol.1 no.2. https://medicine.osu.edu/sitetool
      /sites/pdfs/ahecpublic/Writing_EasytoRead_Materials.pdf.
      Accessed June 21, 2017.

CHAPTER 22

Selected Resources for the Nutrition Professional

Hispanic Culture and Health Statistics

National Alliance for Hispanic Health website. www.hispanichealth.org. Accessed June 26, 2017.

National Center for Health Statistics (NCHS). Health of Hispanic or Latino population. www.cdc.gov/nchs /fastats/hispanic-health.htm. Accessed June 26, 2017.

Salimbene S. *What Language Does Your Patient Hurt In? A Practical Guide to Culturally Competent Care*. 3rd ed. St. Paul, MN: Paradigm Education Solutions; 2015.

US Department of Health and Human Services Office of Minority Health. https://minorityhealth.hhs.gov. Accessed June 26, 2017.

Evaluating the Reading Level of Materials

Doak C, Doak L, Root J. *Teaching Patients with Low Literacy Skills*. 2nd ed. Philadelphia, PA: JB Lippincott; 1996. www.hsph.harvard.edu/healthliteracy /resources/teaching-patients-with-low-literacy-skills.

Dobson B, Betterley C. Guide to evaluating written nutrition materials. Iowa State University Extension, Iowa Department of Public Health. www.health .state.mn.us/divs/fh/wic/localagency/program/mom/ exhbts/ex6/6d2.pdf. Accessed June 26, 2017.

ReadabilityFormulas.com. How to use the SMOG readability formula. www.readabilityformulas .com/articles/how-to-use-smog-readability -formulas-on-health-literacy-materials.php. Accessed June 26, 2017.

The website offers many other resource and readability formulas.

Food and Nutrition

Kittler P, Sucher K. Ethnic ingredients: food composition table. In: *Food and Culture.* Boston, MA: Cengage Learning; 2003. www.cengage.com/resource_uploads /downloads/0538734973_301247.pdf. Accessed June 26, 2017.

Mahan LK, Raymond JL. *Krause's Food and the Nutrition Care Process.* 14th ed. St. Louis, MO: Elsevier; 2017.

Nutrition Care Manual. Resources. Hispanic-English-Spanish Foods Dictionary. www.nutritioncaremanual.org/topic.cfm?ncm _category_id=11&ncm_toc_id=39218&ncm_heading =References&ncm_content_id=92862#References. Accessed June 26, 2017.

Raichlen S. *Steven Raichlen's Healthy Latin Cooking: 200 Sizzling Recipes from Mexico, Cuba, the Caribbean, Brazil, and Beyond.* New York, NY: Rodale Press; 1998.

Rodriguez JC. *Contemporary Nutrition for Latinos.* Lincoln, NE: iUniverse; 2004.

Health Literacy

Centers for Medicare and Medicaid Services. Tools for making written material clear and effective. www.cms.gov/Outreach-and-Education/Outreach /WrittenMaterialsToolkit/index.html?redirect =/WrittenMaterialsToolkit. Accessed June 19, 2017.

Health literacy and patient safety: helping patients understand (video, long version, 23:18 min). American Medical Association Foundation. www.youtube.com /watch?v=cGtTZ_vxjyA. Published August 27, 2010. Accessed November 24, 2017.

Health literacy and patient safety: helping patients understand (video, short version, 4:32 min). American Medical Association Foundation. www.youtube .com/watch?v=BgTuD7l7LG8. Published December 22, 2010. Accessed November 24, 2017.

Health literacy studies. TH Chan School of Public Health, Harvard University. www.hsph.harvard.edu /healthliteracy. Accessed June 19, 2017.

Osborne H. *Health Literacy from A to Z: Practical Ways to Communicate Your Health Message.* 2nd ed. Burlington, MA: Jones & Bartlett Learning; 2013.

Plain Language Action and Information Network website. www.plainlanguage.gov. Accessed June 19, 2017.

Seubert D. A tale of two handouts. applying health literacy principles to improve readability of printed patient education materials. www.health communications.org/resources/handouts.pdf. Accessed June 21, 2017.

Weiss B. *Health Literacy and Patient Safety: Help Patients Understand. A Manual for Clinicians.* 2nd ed. Chicago, IL: American Medical Association Foundation and American Medical Association, 2007. http://med.fsu .edu/userFiles/file/ahec_health_clinicians_manual .pdf. Accessed June 26, 2017.

Nutrition and Health Information Resources for Latino Clients

Academy of Nutrition and Dietetics. *Choose Your Foods: Food List for Diabetes* [Spanish]. www.eatrightstore.org. Accessed June 27, 2017.

Academy of Nutrition and Dietetics. *Choose Your Foods: Plan Your Meals* [Spanish]. www.eatrightstore.org. Accessed June 27, 2017.

American Diabetes Association website [Spanish]. www.diabetes.org/es. Accessed July 7, 2017.

Diabetes Care and Education Dietetic Practice Group of the Academy of Nutrition and Dietetics. *Ready, Set, Start Counting! Carbohydrate Counting: A Tool to Help Manage Your Blood Glucose* [downloadable handout]. English: http://dbcms.s3.amazonaws.com/media/files /84797f22-86a7-4c63-b113-ee51b9759635/1946%20 English%20Handout%20Final.pdf.

Spanish: http://dbcms.s3.amazonaws.com/media/files /b969d11a-78bd-46d6-a54d-bd94983a2944/1946%20 Spanish%20Handout%20NEW.pdf. Accessed October 10, 2017.

National Heart, Lung, and Blood Institute. Latino cardiovascular health resources [English and Spanish]. www.nhlbi.nih.gov/health/health-topics. Accessed June 26, 2017.

Oregon State University Extension Nutrition Education Program. OSU developed educational resources, includes links to Spanish materials. http://extension .oregonstate.edu/nep/osu-edmaterials. Accessed June 26, 2017.

US Department of Agriculture. Information on food and nutrition for consumers, includes links to Spanish materials. www.nutrition.gov. Accessed June 16, 2017.

US Department of Agriculture Center for Nutrition Policy and Promotion. My Plate, My Wins: Make It Yours [poster]. English: https://choosemyplate-prod.azureedge.net /sites/default/files/printablematerials/mini_poster. pdf. Spanish: https://choosemyplate-prod.azureedge.net /sites/default/files/printablematerials/Mini-Poster _Spanish_508_0.pdf. Accessed October 10, 2017.

US Food and Drug Administration. Nutrition Facts Label Program and Materials [Spanish]. www.fda.gov /food/ingredientspackaginglabeling/labeling nutrition/ucm20026097.htm. Accessed June 26, 2017.

For the Nutrition Professional

Always Use Teach-back! training toolkit. www.teachbacktraining.org. Accessed June 26, 2017.

Academy of Nutrition and Dietetics. *Cultural Competency for Nutrition Professionals.* Chicago, IL: Academy of Nutrition and Dietetics; 2016.

Clifford D, Curtis, L. *Motivational Interviewing in Nutrition and Fitness.* New York, NY: The Guildford Press; 2016.

Curry K, Jaffe A. *Nutrition Counseling and Communication Skills.* Philadelphia, PA: WB Saunders; 1998.

Drago L. *15-Minute Consultation Tips: Tools and Activities to Make Your Nutrition Counseling More Effective.* Chicago, IL: Academy of Nutrition and Dietetics; 2016.

Kittler PG, Sucher KP, Nahikian-Nelms M. *Food and Culture.* 7th ed. Boston, MA: Cengage Learning; 2017.

Klinger S, Brogan, K. *Hispanic Family Nutrition: Complete Counseling Kit*. Chicago, IL: Academy of Nutrition and Dietetics; 2016.

Redman BK. *The Practice of Patient Education: A Case Study Approach*. St. Louis, MO: Mosby Elsevier; 2007.

Salimbene S. *What Language Does Your Patient Hurt In? A Practical Guide to Culturally Competent Care*. St Paul, MN: Paradigm Education Solutions; 2015.

Sauter C, Constance A. *Inspiring and Supporting Behavior Change: A Food and Nutrition Professional's Counseling Guide*. 2nd ed. Chicago, IL: Academy of Nutrition and Dietetics; 2017.

APPENDIX A

Spanish Vocabulary for Body Parts

English	Español	Pronunciation
1. head	*cabeza*	ka-BEH-sah
2. eye	*ojo*	OH-hoh
3. ear	*oreja*	oh-REH-hah
4. nose	*nariz*	nah-REES
5. mouth	*boca*	BOH-kah
6. throat	*garganta*	gahr-GAHN-tah
7. arm	*brazo*	BRAH-soh
8. heart	*corazón*	koh-rah-SOHN
9. stomach	*estómago*	ehs-TOH-mah-goh
10. hand	*mano*	MAH-noh
11. leg	*pierna*	pee-EHR-nah
12. foot	*pie*	pee-EH
13. kidney	*riñon*	rreen-YOHN
14. intestine	*intestino*	in-tehs-TEE-noh
15. esophagus	*esófago*	eh-SOH-fah-goh
16. tongue	*lengua*	LEHN-gwah
17. teeth	*dientes*	dee-EHN-tehs
18. pancreas	*páncreas*	PAHN-kree-ahs
19. liver	*hígado*	EEH-gah-thoh
20. colon	*colón*	koh-LOHN
	intestino grueso	ihn-tehs-TEE-noh groo-EH-soh

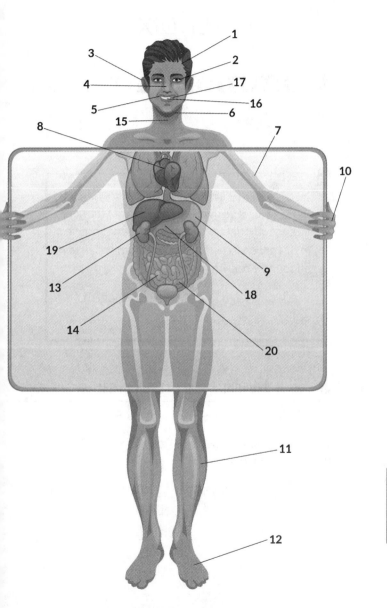

Common Phrases

Some Spanish adjectives can end in either the letter "o" or "a," depending on the gender of the noun that the adjective modifies. These are represented in this appendix with a slash between the oh and ah sound. For example:

boiled   *hervido/a*   ehr-BEE-thoh/thah

See chapter 7 for more details.

English	Español	Pronunciation
Are you . . . ?	*¿Es usted . . . ?*	ehs oo-STEHD . . . ?
Are you breastfeeding?	*¿Está usted amamantando?*	ehs-TAH oo-STEHD ah-mah-mahn-TAHN-doh?
	¿Está usted dando el pecho?	ehs-TAH oo-STEHD DAHN-doh ehl PEH-choh

English	Español	Pronunciation
Are you hungry?	*¿Tiene usted hambre?*	tee-EHN-neh oo-STEHD AHM-breh?
Are you lactose intolerant?	*¿Tiene usted intolerancia a la lactosa?*	tee-EH-neh oo-STEHD een-toh-leh-RAHN-see-ah ah lah lahk-TOH-sah?
Are you pregnant?	*¿Está usted embarazada?*	ehs-TAH oo-STEHD ehm-bah-rah-SAH-thah?
Are you thirsty?	*¿Tiene usted sed?*	tee-EHN-neh oo-STEHD sehd?
Are you using that treatment?	*¿Está usando ese tratamiento?*	eh-STAH oo-SAHN-doh EH-seh trah-tah-mee-EHN-toh?
At 1:00	*A la una*	ah lah OO-nah
At 1:12	*A la una y doce*	ah lah OO-nah ee DOH-seh
	A la una con doce	ah lah OO-nah kohn DOH-seh
At 3:30 in the afternoon	*A las tres y media de la tarde*	ah lahs trehs ee MEH-thee-ah deh lah TAHR-deh
At 7:45 at night	*A las ocho menos cuarto de la noche*	ah lahs OH-choh MEH-nohs KWAHR-toh deh lah NOH-cheh
At 8:00 in the morning	*A las ocho de la mañana*	Ah lahs OH-choh deh lah mahn-YAH-nah

English	Español	Pronunciation
at night	*por la noche*	pohr lah NOH-cheh
	en la noche	ehn lah NOH-cheh
At what time?	*¿A qué hora?*	ah keh OH-rah?
bad for the health	*malo/a para la salud*	MAH-loh/lah pah-rah lah sah-LOOD
blood sugar goal	*meta para azúcar en la sangre*	MEH-tah pah-rah ah-SOO-kahr- ehn lah SAHN-greh
blurry vision	*vista borrosa*	BEES-tah boh-RROH-sah
Could you please speak more slowly?	*¿Podría hablar más despacio, por favor?*	poh-DREE-ah ah-BLAHR mahs des-PAH-see-oh, pohr fah-BOHR?
dairy (like milk, yogurt)	*productos lácteos (como leche, yogur)*	proh-DOOK-tohs LAHK-teh-ohs (KOH-moh LEH-cheh, yoh-GUHR)
desserts and sweets (like churro, buñuelo, candy, cake, sugar-sweetened soda)	*postres y dulces (como churro, buñuelo, caramelos, pastel, refresco con azúcar)*	POHS-trehs ee DUHL-sehs (KOH-moh CHOO-rroh, boon-YWEH-loh, kah-rah-MEH-lohs, pah-STEHL, rreh-FREHS-koh kohn ah-SOO-kahr)
Do you check …?	*¿Revisa usted…?*	rreh-BEE-sah oo-STEHD?

English	Español	Pronunciation
Do you cook?	*¿Usted cocina?*	oo-STEHD koh-SEE-nah?
Do you do...?	*¿Hace usted ...?*	AH-seh oo-STEHD?
Do you drink alcohol?	*¿Toma alcohol?*	TOH-mah ahl-KOHL?
Do you drink milk?	*¿Bebe usted leche?*	BEH-beh oo-STEHD LEH-cheh?
	¿Toma usted leche?	TOH-mah oo-STEHD LEH-cheh?
Do you eat...?	*¿Come usted ...?*	KOH-me oo-STEHD?
Do you exercise?	*¿Hace usted ejercicio?*	AH-seh oo-STEHD eh-hehr-SEE-see-oh?
Do you have...?	*¿Tiene usted ...?*	tee-EH-neh oo-STEHD ...?
Do you have any food allergies?	*¿Le hace daño algún alimento?*	leh ah-seh DAHN-yoh ahl-GOON ah-lee-MEHN-toh?
	¿Tiene (usted) alergia a algún alimento?	tee-EHN-neh oo-STEHD ah-LEHR-hee-ya ah ahl-GOON ah-lee-MEHN-toh?

English	Español	Pronunciation
Do you have problems with your stomach? (heartburn, acid reflux)	*¿Tiene problemas con el estómago? (acidez, reflujo esofágico)*	tee-EH-neh proh-BLEH-mahs kohn ehl eh-STOH-mah-goh? (ah-see-THEHS, rreh-floo-hoh eh-soh-FAH-hee-koh)
Do you like … ?	*¿Le gusta … ?*	leh GOOS-tah … ?
Do you smoke? If so, how often?	*¿Fuma? ¿Si es así, con qué frecuencia?*	FOO-mah? see ehs ah-SEE, kohn keh freh-KWEHN-see-ah?
Do you take any medications?	*¿Toma usted medicamentos?*	TOH-mah oo-STEHD meh-dee-kah-MEHN-tohs?
	¿Toma usted alguna medicación?	TOH-mah oo-STEHD ahl-GOON-ah meh-thee-kah-see-OHN?
Does diabetes run in your family?	*¿Tiene familiares con diabetes?*	tee-EH-neh fah-mee-lee-AH-rehs kohn dee-ah-BEH-tehs?
Does heart disease run in your family?	*¿Tiene familiares con enfermedades del corazón?*	tee-EH-neh fah-mee-lee-AH-rehs kohn ehn-fehr-meh-DAH-thehs dehl koh-rah-SOHN?
Does it have … ?	*¿Tiene … ?*	tee-EH-neh?

English	Español	Pronunciation
every _____ days	*cada _____ días*	kah-thah __ DEE-ahs
every _____ hours	*cada _____ horas*	kah-thah __ OH-rahs
excessive intake	*consumo excesivo*	kohn-SOO-moh ehk-seh-SEE-boh
Foods that contain carbo-hydrates are...	*Comidas que contienen carbohi-dratos son...*	ko-MEE-thahs keh kohn-tee-EH-nehn kahr-boh-ee-DRAH-tohs sohn …
For how long?	*¿Por cuánto tiempo?*	pohr KWAHN-toh tee-EHM-poh?
Good afternoon	*Buenas tardes*	BWEH-nahs TAHR-dehs
Good evening	*Buenas noches*	BWEH-nahs NOH-chehs
good for the health	*bueno/a para la salud*	BWEH-noh/nah pah-rah lah sah-LOOD
Good morning	*Buenos días*	BWEH-nohs DEE-yahs
	Buen día	bwehn DEE-yah
Good-bye	*Adiós*	ah-dee-YOHS
	Chao/Chau	chow
half past	*y media*	ee MEH-thee-yah

English	**Español**	**Pronunciation**
Has anyone ever talked to you about a special diet?	¿Alguna vez alguien le ha sugerido una dieta especial?	ahl-GOON-ah behs AHL-gee-ehn leh ah soo-heh-REE-thoh OO-nah dee-EH-tah eh-speh-see-ahl?
Have you been diagnosed with heart disease, diabetes, hypertension, cancer, or other health problems?	¿Le han diagnosticado con enfermedad del corazón, diabetes, hipertensión, cáncer, u otros problemas de la salud?	leh ahn dee-ahg-noh-stee-KAH-thoh kohn ehn-fehr-meh-THAD dehl koh-rah-SOHN, dee-ah-BEH-tehs, ee-pehr-tehn-see-OHN, KAHN-sehr, oo OH-trohs proh-BLEH-mahs deh lah sah-LOOD?
Have you ever had surgery?	¿Le han operado alguna vez?	leh ahn oh-peh-RAH-thoh ahl-goon-ah BEHS?
Have you gained or lost 5 pounds in the last few months?	¿Ha subido o perdido cinco libras en los últimos pocos meses?	ah soo-BEE-thoh oh pehr-dee-thoh SEEN-koh LEE-brahs ehn lohs OOL-tee-mohs poh-kohs MEH-sehs?
Have you seen a healer or other nonmedical person for your condition?	¿Ha visto un curandero u otra persona que no es médico para su condición?	ah VEES-toh uhn cuh-rahn-DEH-roh oo OH-trah pehr-SOH-nah keh noh ehs MEH-dee-koh PAH-rah soo kohn-dee-see-OHN?

English	Español	Pronunciation
Hello, good morning/ afternoon/ evening	*Hola, buenos días/ tardes/noches*	OH-lah, BWEH-nohs DEE-yahs/TAHR-dehs/ NOH-chehs
high in …	*alto/a en …* *rico/a en …*	AHL-toh/tah ehn RREE-koh/kah ehn
How are you?	*¿Cómo está usted?*	KOH-moh eh-STAH oo-STEHD?
How many alcoholic drinks do you have per day?	*¿Cuántas bebidas alcohólicas toma al día?*	KWAHN-tahs beh-BEE-thahs ahl-KOH-lee-kahs TOH-mah ahl DEE-ah?
How many alcoholic drinks do you have per week?	*¿Cuántas bebidas alcohólicas toma a la semana?*	KWAHN-tahs beh-BEE-thahs ahl-KOH-lee-kahs TOH-mah ah lah seh-MAH-nah?
How many calories does [insert food] have?	*¿Cuántas calorías tiene* [insert food]?	KWAHN-tahs kah-loh-REE-ahs tee-EH-neh [insert food name]?
How much weight have you gained?	*¿Cuánto peso ha aumentado?*	KWAHN-toh PEH-soh ah ow-mehn-TAH-thoh?

English	Español	Pronunciation
How often do you eat in a restaurant?	*¿Con qué frecuencia come en un restaurante?*	kohn keh freh-KWEHN-see-ah KOH-meh ehn oon reh-stow-RAHN-teh?
How old are you?	*¿Cuántos años tiene usted?*	KWAHN-tohs AHN-yohs tee-EH-neh oo-STEHD?
	¿Qué edad tiene usted?	keh eh-DAD tee–EH-neh oo-STEHD?
How tall are you?	*¿Qué altura tiene?*	keh ahl-TOO-rah tee-EH-neh?
I am …	*Soy …*	Soy …
I am from …	*(Yo) soy de …*	(yoh) soy deh …
I am full.	*(Yo) estoy satis-fecho/a.*	(yoh) ehs-TOY sah-tees-FEH-choh/ah.
I am hungry.	*(Yo) tengo hambre.*	(yoh) TEHN-goh AHM-breh
I am pregnant.	*Estoy embarazada.*	ehs-TOY ehm-bah-rah-SAH-thah
I am thirsty.	*(Yo) tengo sed.*	(yoh) TEHN-goh sehd
I cannot eat dairy products.	*Me hacen daño los productos lácteos.*	meh AH-sehn DAHN-yoh lohs proh-DOOK-tohs LAHK-teh-ohs
I don't eat …	*(Yo) no como …*	(yoh) noh KOH-moh

English	Español	Pronunciation
I don't like to eat…	*No me gusta comer…*	noh meh-GOOS-tah koh-MEHR…
I eat…	*(Yo) como…*	(yoh) KOH-moh
I have…	*Tengo…*	TEHN-goh…
I like to eat…	*Me gusta comer…*	meh-GOOS-tah koh-MEHR…
I weigh _____ pounds.	*Peso_____ libras.*	PEH-soh___ LEE-brahs
I'm _____ years old.	*Tengo _____ años.*	tehn-goh ___AHN-yohs
I'm sorry, but I speak very little Spanish.	*Lo siento, pero hablo muy poco español.*	loh see-YEHN-toh, PEH-roh AH-bloh moo-wee POH-koh eh-spahn-YOHL
If so, what for?	*¿Si es así, qué tipo de operación?*	see ehs ah-SEE, keh TEE-poh theh oh-peh-rah-see-OHN?
If so, what type and how often?	*Si es que sí, ¿de qué tipo y con qué frecuencia?*	see ehs keh see, deh keh TEE-poh ee kohn keh freh-KWEHN-see-ah?
If so, what was the health problem?	*¿Si es así, cuál fue el problema de salud?*	see ehs ah-SEE, KWAHL fweh ehl proh-BLEH-mah deh sah-LOOD?

English	Español	Pronunciation
in order to gain weight	*para subir de peso*	pah-rah soo-BEER deh PEH-soh
	para engordar	pah-rah ehn-gohr-DAHR
in order to lose weight	*para perder peso*	pah-rah pehr-DEHR PEH-soh
	para bajar de peso	pah-rah bah-HAHR deh PEH-soh
	para adelgazar	pah-rah ah-dehl-gah-SAHR
in the afternoon	*por la tarde*	pohr lah TAHR-deh
	en la tarde	ehn lah TAHR-deh
in the morning	*por la mañana*	pohr lah mahn-YAH-nah
	en la mañana	ehn lah mahn-YAH-nah
It has …	*Tiene…*	tee-EH-neh
It would be good for you to eat every 3 hours.	*Usted debiera comer cada tres horas.*	oo-STEHD deh-bee-EH-rah koh-MEHR kah-thah trehs OH-rahs.
It's good to (you should) drink plenty of water every day.	*Usted debiera beber bastante agua cada día.*	oo-STEHD deh-bee-EH-rah beh-BEHR bahs-TAHN-teh AH-gwah kah-thah DEE-ah.

English	Español	Pronunciation
It's good to (you should) eat [insert number] portions of [insert food].	*Usted debiera comer* [insert number] *porciones de* [insert type of food].	oo-STEHD deh-bee-EH-rah koh-MEHR [insert number] pohr-see-OH-nehs deh [insert type of food].
It's good to (you should) eat five fruits and vegetables a day.	*Usted debiera comer cinco frutas y vegetales cada día.*	oo-STEHD deh-bee-EH-rah koh-MEHR SEEN-koh FROO-tahs ee beh-heh-TAH-lehs kah-thah DEE-ah.
low in . . .	*bajo/a en . . .*	BAH-hoh/hah ehn
(in) moderation	*(con) moderación*	(kohn) moh-deh-rah-see-OHN
My name is . . .	*Me llamo . . .*	meh YAH-moh . . .
	Mi nombre es . . .	mee NOHM-breh ehs . . .
No, I am not breastfeeding.	*No, no estoy amamantando.*	noh, noh ehs-TOY ah-mah-mahn-TAHN-doh
	No, no estoy dando el pecho.	Noh, noh ehs-TOY DAHN-doh ehl PEH-choh
No, I don't like . . .	*No, no me gusta . . .*	no, noh meh GOOS-tah . . .
Not very well	*No muy bien*	noh moo-wee bee-EHN

English	Español	Pronunciation
Pleased to meet you	*Encantada* [only used by females, to people of both genders]	ehn-kahn-TAH-thah
	Encantado [only used by males, to people of both genders]	ehn-kahn-TAH-thoh
	Mucho gusto	MOO-choh GOO-stoh
quarter after	*y cuarto*	ee KWAHR-toh
See you later.	*Hasta luego.*	AH-stah loo-WEH-goh.
	Hasta la vista.	AH-stah lah VEE-stah.
See you next time.	*Hasta la próxima.*	AH-stah lah PROHK-see-mah.
See you soon	*Hasta pronto.*	AH-stah PROHN-toh.
See you tomorrow	*Hasta mañana*	AH-stah mahn-YAH-nah
Should I lose weight?	*¿Debo perder peso?*	DEH-boh pehr-dehr PEH-soh?
	¿Debo bajar de peso?	DEH-boh bah-HAHR deh PEH-soh?
small piece(s)	*trocito(s)*	troh-SEE-toh(s)
	pedacito(s)	peh-thah-SEE-toh(s)

English	Español	Pronunciation
So-so	*Así, así*	ah-SEE, ah-SEE
	Más o menos	mahs oh MEH-nohs
starchy vegetables (like corn or potatoes)	*verduras ricas en almidón (como maíz o papas)*	behr-DOO-rahs RREE-kahs ehn ahl-mee-DOHN (KOH-moh mah-EES oh PAH-pahs)
Tell me what you usually eat for breakfast, for lunch, for dinner, for snacks.	*Dígame lo que usualmente come para el desayuno, el almuerzo, la cena y como merienda.*	DEE-gah-meh loh keh oo-soo-ahl-MEHN-teh KO-meh pah-rah ehl deh-sah-OO-noh, ehl ahl-MWEHR-soh, lah SEH-nah ee koh-moh meh-ree-EHN-dah
Thank you, and you?	*Gracias, ¿y usted?*	GRAH-see-ahs, ee oo-STEHD?
to go on a diet	*ponerse a dieta*	poh-NEHR-seh ah dee-EH-tah
	ponerse a régimen	poh-NEHR-seh ah RREH-hee-mehn
too much	*demasiado/a excesivo/a*	deh-mah-see-AH-thoh/thah ehk-seh-SEE-boh/bah
units of insulin	*unidades de insulina*	oo-nee-DAH-thehs deh een-soo-LEE-nah

English	Español	Pronunciation
Vegetables are high in fiber and low in fat.	*Los vegetales son altos en fibra y bajos en grasa.*	lohs beh-heh-TAH-lehs sohn AHL-tohs ehn FEE-brah ee BAH-hohs ehn GRAH-sah.
We'll see each other	*Nos vemos*	nohs BEH-mohs
What can I drink?	*¿Qué puedo beber?*	keh PWEH-thoh beh-BEHR?
	¿Qué puedo tomar?	keh PWEH-thoh toh-MAHR?
What can't I drink?	*¿Qué no puedo beber?*	keh noh PWEH-thoh beh-BEHR?
	¿Qué no puedo tomar?	keh noh PWEH-thoh toh-MAHR?
What can't I eat?	*¿Qué no puedo comer?*	keh noh PWEH-thoh koh-MEHR?
What country are you from?	*¿De qué país es usted?*	deh keh pah-EES ehs oo-STEHD?
What did this person recommend?	*¿Qué le recomendó esa persona?*	keh leh reh-koh-mehn-DOH EH-sah pehr-SOH-nah?

English	Español	Pronunciation
What do I need to drink?	*¿Qué necesito tomar?*	keh neh-seh-SEE-toh toh-MAHR?
	¿Qué necesito beber?	keh neh-seh-SEE-toh beh-BEHR?
What do I need to eat?	*¿Qué necesito comer?*	keh neh-seh-SEE-toh koh-MEHR?
What do you like to eat?	*¿Qué le gusta comer (a usted)?*	keh leh GOOS-tah koh-MEHR (ah oo-STEHD)?
What do you usually weigh?	*¿Cuánto pesa usted normalmente?*	KWAHN-toh PEH-sah oo-STEHD nohr-mahl-MEHN-teh?
What don't you like to eat?	*¿Qué no le gusta comer (a usted)?*	keh noh leh GOOS-tah koh-MEHR (ah oo-STEHD)?
What herbs or diet supplements do you take now?	*¿Toma usted algún suplemento dietético o té de hierbas?*	TOH-mah oo-STEHD ahl-GOON soo-pleh-MEHN-toh dee-eh-TEH-tee-koh oh teh theh yee-EHR-bahs?
What is your name?	*¿Cómo se llama usted?*	KOH-moh seh YAH-mah oo-STEHD?
	¿Cuál es su nombre?	kwahl ehs soo NOHM-breh?

English	Español	Pronunciation
What kind?	*¿Qué clase?*	keh KLAH-seh?
	¿Qué tipo?	keh TEE-poh?
	¿De cuál?	deh KWAHL?
What should I drink?	*¿Qué debo beber?*	keh DEH-boh beh-BEHR?
	¿Qué debo tomar?	keh DEH-boh toh-MAHR?
What should I eat?	*¿Qué debo comer?*	keh DEH-boh koh-MEHR?
What shouldn't I drink?	*¿Qué no debo beber?*	keh noh DEH-boh beh-BEHR?
	¿Qué no debo tomar?	keh noh DEH-boh toh-MAHR?
What shouldn't I eat?	*¿Qué no debo comer?*	keh noh DEH-boh koh-MEHR?
What was your prepregnancy weight?	*¿Cuánto pesaba usted antes de quedar embarazada?*	KWAHN-toh peh-SAH-bah oo-STEHD AHN-tehs deh keh-THAHR ehm-bah-rah-SAH-thah?
What/which do you take?	*¿Cuál toma (usted)?*	kwahl TOH-mah oo-STEHD
When are you due to deliver?	*¿Cuándo va a dar a luz?*	KWAHN-doh bah ah dahr ah- LOOS?
	¿Cuándo va a aliviarse?	KWAHN-doh bah ah ah-lee-bee-AHR-seh?

English	Español	Pronunciation
When?	*¿Cúando?*	KWAHN-doh?
Which of the carbohydrate foods are most important to you?	*¿Cuáles de las comidas que contienen carbohidratos le importan más?*	KWAH-lehs deh lahs koh-MEE-thahs keh kohn-tee-EH-nehn kahr-boh-ee-DRAH-tohs leh eem-POHR-tahn MAHS?
Who buys the food you eat?	*¿Quién compra la comida que come?*	kee-EHN KOHM-prah lah koh-MEE-thah keh KOH-meh?
With what symptoms?	*¿Qué sintomas le da?*	keh SEEN-toh-mahs leh dah?
Yes, I am breastfeeding.	*Sí, estoy amamantando.*	see, ehs-TOY ah-mah-mahn-TAHN-doh
	Sí, estoy dando el pecho.	see, ehs-TOY DAHN-doh ehl PEH-choh
Yes, I like …	*Sí, me gusta …*	see, meh GOOS-tah …
Yes, I take …	*Sí, tomo …*	see, TOH-moh …
You can drink …	*Usted puede beber …*	oo-STEHD PWEH-theh beh-BEHR …
	Usted puede tomar …	oo-STEHD PWEH-theh toh-MAHR …
You can eat …	*Usted puede comer …*	oo-STEHD PWEH-theh koh-MEHR …

English	Español	Pronunciation
You need to drink...	*Usted necesita beber...*	oo-STEHD neh-seh-SEE-tah beh-BEHR...
You need to eat...	*Usted necesita comer...*	oo-STEHD neh-seh-SEE-tah koh-MEHR...

English	Español	Pronunciation
You should drink...	*Usted debiera beber...*	oo-STEHD deh-bee-EH-rah beh-BEHR...
	Usted debiera tomar...	oo-STEHD deh-bee-EH-rah toh-MAHR...
You should eat...	*Usted debiera comer...*	oo-STEHD deh-bee-EH-rah koh-MEHR...
You should not drink...	*Usted no debiera beber...*	oo-STEHD noh deh-bee-EH-rah beh-BEHR...
	Usted no debiera tomar...	oo-STEHD noh deh-bee-EH-rah toh-MAHR...
You should not eat...	*Usted no debiera comer...*	oo-STEHD noh deh-bee-EH-rah koh-MEHR...
You shouldn't drink...	*Usted no debiera beber...*	oo-STEHD noh deh-bee-EH-rah beh-BEHR...
	Usted no debiera tomar...	oo-STEHD noh deh-bee-EH-rah toh-MAHR...

English to Spanish Glossary

> *Some Spanish adjectives can end in either the letter "o" or "a," depending on the gender of the noun that the adjective modifies. These are represented in this appendix with a slash between the oh and ah sound. For example:*
>
> boiled   *hervido/a*   ehr-BEE-thoh/thah
>
> *See chapter 7 for more details.*

Numbers

zero	*cero*	SEH-roh
one	*uno*	OO-noh
two	*dos*	dohs
three	*tres*	trehs

four	*cuatro*	KWAH-troh
five	*cinco*	SEEN-koh
six	*seis*	SEH-ees
seven	*siete*	see-EH-teh
eight	*ocho*	OH-choh
nine	*nueve*	noo-EH-beh
ten	*diez*	dee-ehs
eleven	*once*	OHN-seh
twelve	*doce*	DOH-seh
thirteen	*trece*	TREH-seh
fourteen	*catorce*	kah-TOHR-seh
fifteen	*quince*	KEEN-seh
twenty	*veinte*	BEHN-teh
thirty	*treinta*	TREHN-tah
forty	*cuarenta*	kwah-REHN-tah
fifty	*cincuenta*	seen-KWEHN-tah
sixty	*sesenta*	seh-SEHN-tah
seventy	*setenta*	seh-TEHN-tah
eighty	*ochenta*	oh-CHEHN-tah

ninety	*noventa*	noh-BEHN-tah
one hundred	*cien*	see-EHN
	ciento	see-EHN-toh
two hundred	*doscientos*	dohs-see-EHN-tohs
three hundred	*trescientos*	trehs-see-EHN-tohs
four hundred	*cuatrocientos*	kwah-troh-see-EHN-tohs
five hundred	*quinientos*	kee-nee-YEHN-tohs
six hundred	*seiscientos*	see-ehs-see-EHN-tohs
seven hundred	*setecientos*	seh-teh-see-EHN-tohs
eight hundred	*ochocientos*	oh-choh-see-EHN-tohs
nine hundred	*novecientos*	noh-beh-see-EHN-tohs
one thousand	*mil*	meel
two thousand	*dos mil*	dohs meel
three thousand	*tres mil*	trehs meel

A

about (with time or numbers)	*más o menos*	mahs oh MEH-nohs
achiote (seasoning paste made from annatto seeds)	*achiote*	ah-chee-YOH-teh
almonds	*almendras*	ahl-MEHN-drahs
always	*siempre*	see-EHM-preh
American cheese	*queso americano*	KEH-soh ah-meh-ree-KAH-noh
anemia	*anemia*	ah-NEH-mee-ah
anorexia (nervosa)	*anorexia (nerviosa)*	ah-noh-REK-see-ah (nehr-bee-OH sah)
anorexic	*anoréxico/a*	ah-noh-REK-see-koh/kah
appetizer	*antojito*	ahn-toh-HEE-toh
	aperitivo	ah-peh-ree-TEE-boh
	entrada	ehn-TRAH-thah
apple	*manzana*	mahn-SAH-nah

apple juice	*jugo de manzana*	HOO-goh deh mahn-SAH-nah
approximately	*aproximadamente*	ah-PROHK-see-mah-thah MEHN-teh
apricot	*albaricoque*	ahl-bah-ree-KOH-keh
	damasco	dah-MAHS-koh
	chabacano	chah-bah-KAH-noh
around	*más o menos*	mahs oh MEH-nohs
artificial sweetener	*endulzante (artificial)*	ehn-dool-SAHN-teh (ahr-tee-fee-see-AHL)
avocado	*aguacate*	ah-gwah-KAH-teh
	palta	PAHL-tah

B

bacon	*tocino*	toh-SEE-noh
	tocineta	toh-see-NEH-tah
	panceta	pahn-SEH-tah
bad	*mal*	mahl
baked	*al horno*	ahl OHR-noh
	horneado/a	ohr-neh-AH-thoh/ah

banana	*plátano*	PLAH-tah-noh
	banana	bah-NAH-nah
	banano	bah-NAH-noh
	guineo	ghee-NEH-oh
barbecued meat	*barbacoa*	bahr-bah-KOH-ah
	picada	pee-KAH-thah
	al carbón	ahl kahr-BOHN
barley	*cebada*	seh-BAH-thah
beans	*frijoles*	free-HOH-lehs
	habichuelas	ah-bee-CHWEH-lahs
	porotos	poh-ROH-tohs
beef	*carne de res*	KAHR-neh deh RREHS
	carne roja	KAHR-neh RROH-hah
beer	*cerveza*	sehr-BEH-sah
beet	*remolacha*	rreh-moh-LAH-chah
	betabel	beh-tah-BEHL
beverage	*bebida*	beh-BEE-thah
blackberry	*mora*	MOH-rah
blanch	*blanquear*	blahn-keh-AHR
	escaldar	ehs-kahl-DAHR

blood	*sangre*	SAHN-greh
blue cheese	*queso azul*	KEH-soh ah-SOOL
blueberries	*arándanos (azules)*	ah-RAHN-dah-nohs (ah-SOO-lehs)
boiled	*hervido/a*	ehr-BEE-thoh/thah
bowel movement/ feces	*excremento*	eks-kreh-MEHN-toh
	popo	POH-poh
	caca (informal)	KAH-kah
braise	*estofar*	eh-stoh-FAHR
bran	*salvado*	sahl-BAH-thoh
bread	*pan*	pahn
bread roll	*bolillo*	boh-LEE-yoh
	panecillo	pah-neh-SEE-yoh
breakfast	*desayuno*	deh-sah-YOO-noh
breast pump	*sacaleche*	sah-kah-LEH-cheh
	extractor de leche materna	ehk-strahk-TOHR deh LEH-cheh mah-TERN-nah
broccoli	*broccoli*	BROH-koh-lee
	brécol	BREH-kohl
broiled	*a la parrilla*	ah lah pah-RREE-yah

brown rice	*arroz integral*	ah-RROHS een-teh-GRAHL
	arroz moreno	ah-RROHS moh-REH-noh
brush (pan with oil)	*pincelar asadera con aceite*	peen-seh-LAHR ah-sah-THEH-rah kohn ah-see-EH-teh
	untar aceite al molde de hornear	uhn-TAHR ah-SEH-ee-teh ahl MOHL-deh deh ohr-neh-AHR
brussels sprouts	*col de Bruselas*	kohl deh broo-SEH-lahs
	bruselas	broo-SEH-lahs
	repollitos de Bruselas	rreh-poh-YEE-tohs deh broo-SEH-lahs
	colecitas de Bruselas	koh-leh-SEE-tahs deh broo-SEH-lahs
bulimia (nervosa)	*bulimia (nerviosa)*	boo-LEE-mee-ah (nehr-bee-OH-sah)
bulimic	*bulímico/a*	boo-LEE-mee-koh/kah
butter (can also refer to lard)	*mantequilla*	mahn-teh-KEE-yah
	manteca	mahn-TEH-kah
	grasa animal	GRAH-sah ah-nee-MAHL
	grasa de cerdo	GRAH-sah theh SEHR-doh
buttermilk	*suero*	SWEH-roh

C

cabbage	*col*	kohl
	repollo	rreh-POH-yoh
cactus	*nopal*	noh-PAHL
	nopalitos	noh-pah-LEE-tohs
cake	*pastel*	pah-STEHL
	torta	TOHR-tah
	bizcocho	bees-KOH-choh
calorie(s)	*caloría(s)*	kah-loh-REE-ah(s)
candy	*dulces*	DOOL-sehs
	caramelos	kah-rah-MEH-lohs
	golosinas	goh-loh-SEE-nahs
canned	*en lata*	ehn LAH-tah
	enlatado/a	ehn-lah-TAH-thoh/thah
canola oil	*aceite de canola*	ah-SEH-ee-teh theh kah-NOH-lah
cantaloupe	*cantalupo*	kahn-tah-LOO-poh
	melón	meh-LOHN
carbohy-drate(s)	*carbohidrato(s)*	kahr-boh-ee-DRAH-toh(s)

carrots	*zanahorias*	sah-nah-OH-ree-yahs
cashews	*anacardos*	ah-nah-KAHR-thos
	castaña de cajú	kahs-TAHN-yah deh kah-HOO
	marañones	mah-rahn-YOH-nes
cauliflower	*coliflor*	koh-lee-FLOHR
celery	*apio*	AH-pee-oh
cereal	*cereal*	seh-reh-AHL
	maizoro	mah-ee-SOH-roh
cheddar cheese	*queso cheddar*	KEH-soh CHEH-thar
cheese	*queso*	KEH-soh
cherries	*cerezas*	seh-REH-sahs
chicken	*pollo*	POH-yoh
chili pepper	*chile*	CHEE-leh
chili powder (contains garlic and cumin)	*chile en polvo*	CHEE-leh ehn POHL-boh
chili with meat	*chile con carne*	CHEE-leh kohn KAHR-neh

chips (snack chips)	*chips*	cheeps
	totopos	toh-TOH-pohs
	papitas de bolsa	pah-PEE-tahs deh BOHL-sah
	papitas fritas	pah-PEE-tahs FREE-tahs
	tostaditas	toh-stah-THEE-tahs
chocolate	*chocolate*	choh-koh-LAH-teh
chocolate milk	*leche de chocolate*	LEH-cheh deh choh-koh-LAH-teh
	leche chocolate	LEH-cheh choh-koh-LAH-teh
	leche con Quik	LEH-cheh kohn KWEEK
	leche achocolatada	LEH-cheh ah-choh-koh-lah-TAH-thah
cholesterol	*colesterol*	koh-lehs-teh-ROHL
chopped	*picado/a*	pee-KAH-thoh/thah
	troceado/a	troh-seh-AH-thoh/thah
cilantro/ coriander	*cilandro*	see-LAHND-roh
	culantro	koo-LAHN-troh
	coriandro	koh-ree-AHN-droh
	cilantro	see-LAHN-troh

cinnamon	*canela*	kah-NEH-lah
clams	*almejas*	ahl-MEH-hahs
clove (of garlic)	*diente (de ajo)*	dee-EHN-teh (deh AH-hoh)
coconut	*coco*	KOH-koh
coconut milk	*leche de coco*	LEH-cheh deh KOH-koh
coffee	*café*	kah-FEH
coffee with milk and sugar	*café con leche*	kah-FEH kohn LEH-cheh
cold	*frío/a*	free-oh/free-ah
cold cuts	*carne para sándwich*	KAHR-neh pah-rah SAHND-weech
	embutidos	ehm-boo-TEE-thohs
cole slaw	*ensalada de col*	ehn-sah-LAH-thah deh KOHL
	ensalada de repollo	ehn-sah-LAH-thah deh reh-POH-yoh
colostrum	*calostro*	cah-LOH-stroh

constipation	*estreñimiento*	ehs-trehn-yee-mee-EHN-toh
	constipación	kohn-stee-pah-see-OHN
	sequedad de vientre	seh-keh-THAD theh bee-EHN-treh
cooked	*cocido/a*	koh-SEE-thoh/thah
cookies	*galletas*	gah-YEH-tahs
	dulces	DOOL-sehs
coriander	*cilandro*	see-LAHND-roh
	culantro	koo-LAHN-troh
	coriandro	koh-ree-AHN-droh
	cilantro	see-LAHN-troh
corn	*maíz*	mah-EES
	elote	eh-LOH-teh
corn husk	*oja*	OH-hah
	hoja de maíz	OH-hah theh mah-EES
	hoja	OH-hah
corn oil	*aceite de maíz*	ah-SEH-ee-teh deh mah-EES

corn on the cob	*elote*	eh-LOH-teh
	mazorca de maíz	mah-SOHR-kah deh mah-EES
	choclo de maíz	CHOH-kloh deh mah-EES
corn tortilla	*tortilla de maiz*	tohr-TEE-yah deh mah-EES
cottage cheese	*requesón*	rreh-keh-SOHN
	queso blanco grumoso	KEH-soh BLAHN-koh groo-MOH-soh
cranberries	*arándanos rojos (y agrios)*	ah-RAHN-dah-nohs RROH-hohs (ee AH-gree-ohs)
cranberry juice	*jugo de arándano agrio*	HOO-goh deh ah-RAHN-dah-noh AH-gree-yoh
cream	*nata*	NAH-tah
	crema	KREH-mah
cream cheese	*queso crema*	KEH-soh KREH-mah
cube(s)	*cubo(s)*	KOO-boh(s)
	cubitos	koo-BEE-tohs
cucumber	*pepino*	peh-PEE-noh
cumin	*comino*	koh-MEE-noh
cup(s)	*taza(s)*	TAH-sah(s)
	tazas de medir	TAH-sahs deh meh-DEER

cupcake	*pastelito*	pahs-teh-LEE-toh
	magdalena	mahg-dah-LEH-nah
	cubilete	koo-bee-LEH-teh
	mantecada	mahn-teh-KAH-thah
	pastelillo	pahs-teh-LEE-yoh
	bizcochito	bees-koh-CHEE-toh
custard	*flan*	flahn
cut up	*cortado/a*	kohr-TAH-thoh/thah

D

dairy	*productos lácteos*	proh-DOOK-tohs LAHK-teh-ohs
dark-green leafy vegetables	*verduras de hojas verdes*	behr-DOO-rahs deh OH-hahs BEHR-thehs)
date	*dátil*	DAH-teel
debone	*deshuesar*	dehs-weh-SAHR
desserts	*postres*	POHS-trehs
devein	*deshuesar*	dehs-weh-SAHR
diabetes	*diabetes*	dee-ah-BEH-tehs

diarrhea	*diarrea*	dee-ah-RREH-ah
diet	*dieta*	dee-EH-tah
diet soft drink	*refresco de dieta*	rreh-FREHS-koh deh dee-EH-tah
	gaseosa de dieta	gah-seh-OH-sah deh dee-EH-tah
	refresco lite	rreh-FREHS-koh LAHYT
	gaseosa lite	gah-seh-OH-sah LAHYT
difficulty chewing	*problemas al masticar*	proh-BLE-mahs ahl mahs-tee-KAHR
difficulty swallowing	*problemas al tragar*	proh-BLE-mahs ahl trah-GAHR
dinner	*cena*	SEH-nah
disease	*enfermedad*	ehn-fehr-meh-DAHD
disorder	*trastorno*	trahs-TOHR-noh
donuts	*donas*	DOH-nahs
	rosquillas	rroh-SKEE-yahs
drink	*bebida*	beh-BEE-thah
dry	*seco*	SEH-koh
duck	*pato*	PAH-toh

E

egg omelet	*tortilla francesa*	tohr-TEE-ya frahn-SEH-sah
	tortilla de huevo	tohr-TEE-ya deh WEH-boh
egg white	*clara de huevo*	KLAH-rah deh WEH-boh
	clara de blanquillo	KLAH-rah deh blahn-KEE-yoh
egg yolk	*yema de huevo*	YEH-mah deh WEH-boh
	yema de blanquillo	YEH-mah deh blahn-KEE-yoh
eggplant	*berenjena*	beh-rehn-HEH-nah
eggs	*huevos*	WEH-bohs
	blanquillos	blahn-KEE-yohs
eggs, scrambled	*huevos revueltos*	WEH-bohs rreh-BWEHL-tohs
energy	*energía*	eh-nehr-HEE-ah
evaporated milk	*leche evaporada*	LEH-cheh eh-bah-poh-RAH-thah

F

fat	*grasa*	GRAH-sah
fat-free	*sin grasa*	seen GRAH-sah

feet/foot	*pie/pies*	pee-EH/pee-EHS
fiber	*fibra*	FEE-brah
fig	*higo*	EE-goh
fine	*bien*	bee-EHN
fish	*pescado*	peh-SKAH-thoh
flavored water	*agua saborizada*	AH-gwah sah-boh-ree-SAH-thah
	agua de sabor	AH-gwah deh sah-BOR
flatulence	*gases*	GAH-sehs
	flatulencia	flah-too-LEHN-see-ah
flour	*harina*	ah-REE-nah
flour tortilla	*tortilla de harina*	tohr-TEE-yah deh ah-REE-nah
folic acid	*ácido fólico*	AH-see-thoh FOH-lee-koh
french fries	*papas fritas*	PAH-pahs FREE-tahs
	papitas	pah-PEE-tahs
french toast	*tostada francesa*	tohs-TAH-thah frahn-SEH-sah
	torrija	tohr-rree-hah
	torreja	tohr-rreh-hah
fresh	*fresco/a*	FREHS-koh/kah

fresh cheese	*queso fresco*	KEH-soh FREHS-koh
Friday	*viernes*	bee-YEHR-nehs
fried	*frito/a*	FREE-toh/tah
frozen	*congelado/a*	kohn-heh-LAH-thoh/thah
fruit juice	*jugo de frutas*	HOO-goh deh FROO-tahs
fruits	*frutas*	FROO-tahs

G

garlic	*ajo*	AH-hoh
garlic clove	*diente de ajo*	dee-EHN-teh deh AH-hoh
garlic salt	*sal de ajo*	sahl deh AH-hoh
gas	*gases*	GAH-sehs
	flatulencia	flah-too-LEHN-see-ah
gelatin	*gelatina*	heh-lah-TEE-nah
generally	*generalmente*	heh-neh-rahl-MEHN-teh
gestational diabetes	*diabetes gestacional*	dee-ah-BEH-tehs hehs-tah-see-oh-NAHL
	diabetes del embarazo	dee-ah-BEH-tehs dehl ehm-bah-RAH-soh
gizzards	*mollejas*	moh-YEH-hahs

gluten allergy	*alergia al gluten*	ah-LEHR-hee-ah ahl GLOO-tehn
grains	*granos*	GRAH-nohs
gram(s)	*gramo(s)*	GRAH-moh(s)
grape juice	*jugo de uva*	HOO-goh deh OO-bah
grapefruit	*toronja*	toh-ROHN-hah
	pomelo	poh-MEH-loh
grapes	*uvas*	OO-bahs
grate	*rallar*	rrah-YAHR
green beans	*judías verdes*	hoo-THEE-ahs BEHR-dehs
	ejotes	eh-HOH-tehs
	porotos verdes	poh-ROH-tehs BEHR-dehs
	habichuelas verdes	ah-bee-CHWEH-lahs behr-thehs
green bell pepper	*pimiento verde*	pee-mee-EHN-toh BEHR-deh
	chile verde	CHEE-leh BEHR-deh
	aji verde	ah-HEE BEHR-deh
	chile ancho	CHEE-leh AHN-choh
	pimiento dulce	pee-mee-EHN-toh DOOHL-seh

green onion/ scallion	*cebolla de verdeo*	seh-BOH-yah theh behr-THEH-oh
	cebolla larga	seh-BOH-yah LAHR-gah
	cebolleta	seh-BOH-YEH-tah
green peas	*guisantes*	ghee-SAHN-tehs
	chícharos	CHEE-chah-rohs
	petit pois	peh-tee PWAH
grilled	*asado/a*	ah-SAH-thoh/thah
grilled beef	*carne asada*	KAHR-neh ah-SAH-thah
	carne a la tampiqueña	KAHR-neh ah lah tahm-pee-KEHN-yah
	carne a la plancha	KAHR-neh ah lah PLAHN-chah
grilled cheese sandwich	*sándwich de queso fundido*	SAHND-weech deh KEH-soh foon-DEE-thoh
	sándwich de queso derretido	SAHND-weech deh KEH-soh deh-rreh-TEE-thoh
ground beef	*carne molida*	KAHR-neh moh-LEE-thah
	carne picada	KAHR-neh pee-KAH-thah
guava	*guava*	GWAH-bah
	guayaba or *guayava*	gwah-YAH-bah

H

half	*media*	MEH-thee-ah
	mitad	mee-TAHD
ham	*jamón*	hah-MOHN
hamburger	*hamburguesa*	ahm-boor-GEH-sah
hash (with meat)	*picadillo*	pee-kah-DEE-yoh
hash browns	*papas doradas*	PAH-pahs doh-rah-thahs
hazelnuts	*avellanas*	ah-beh-YEHN-ahs
headaches	*dolores de cabeza*	doh-LOH-rehs deh kah-BEH-sah
healthy	*sano*	SAH-noh
	saludable	sah-loo-DAH-bleh
heart	*corazón*	koh-rah-SOHN
heartburn/ acid reflux	*acidéz/reflujo ácido*	ah-see-THEHS/rreh-FLOO-hoh AH-see-thoh
herbs	*hierbas*	YEHR-bahs
high blood pressure	*presión (arterial) alta*	preh-see-OHN (ahr-teh-ree-AHL) AHL-tah
	alta presión	AHL-tah preh-see-OHN
high cholesterol	*colesterol alto*	koh-lehs-teh-ROHL AHL-toh

honey	*miel de abeja*	mee-YEHL deh ah-BEH-hah
hot (temperature)	*caliente*	kah-lee-EHN-teh
hot chocolate	*chocolate*	choh-koh-LAH-teh
hot dog	*salchicha*	sahl-CHEE-chah
	hot dog	HOHT dohg
	pancho	PAHN-choh
how many	*cuántos/as*	KWAHN-tohs/tahs
hunger	*hambre*	AHM-breh
hyperglyce-mia	*hiperglucemia*	ee-pehr-gloo-SEH-mee-yah
hypoglycemia	*hipoglucemia*	ee-poh-gloo-SEH-mee-yah

I

ice cream	*helado*	eh-LAH-thoh
	nieve	nee-EH-beh
	mantecado	mahn-teh-KAH-thoh
iced tea	*té helado*	teh eh-LAH-thoh
	té frío	teh FREE-oh
indigestion	*indigestión*	een-dee-heh-stee-OHN
iron	*hierro*	ee-EH-rroh

J

jelly	*jalea*	hah-LEH-yah
	mermelada	mehr-meh-LAH-thah
	dulce	DOOL-seh
	ate	AH-teh
jicama	*jícama*	HEE-kah-mah
juice	*jugo*	HOO-goh
	zumo	THOO-moh

K

ketchup	*catsup*	KAHT-soop
	salsa de tomate	SAHL-sah deh toh-MAH-teh
	salsa de jitomate	SAHL-sah deh hee- toh-MAH-teh
kidneys	*riñones*	rreen-YOH-nehs
kiwi	*kiwi*	KEE-wee

L

| label | *etiqueta* | eh-tee-KEH-tah |
| lactose intolerance | *intolerancia a la lactosa* | een-toh-leh-RAHN-see-ah ah lah lahk-TOH-sah |

lamb	*cordero*	kohr-THEH-roh
	carnero	kahr-NEH-roh
lancet	*lanceta*	lahn-SEH-tah
lard	*manteca*	mahn-TEH-kah
	grasa animal	GRAH-sah ah-nee-MAHL
	grasa de cerdo	GRAH-sah deh SEHR-doh
latch on (for breast-feeding)	*prenderse*	prehn-DEHR-seh
leek	*puerro*	PWEH-rroh
legumes	*legumbres*	leh-GOOM-brehs
lemon	*limón*	lee-MOHN
	lima	LEE-mah
lemonade	*limonada*	lee-moh-NAH-thah
lentils	*lentejas*	lehn-TEH-hahs
less	*menos*	MEH-nohs
lettuce	*lechuga*	leh-CHOO-gah
lime	*lima*	LEE-mah
	limón	lee-MOHN
liver	*hígado*	EE-gah-thoh

liver disease	*enfermedad del hígado*	ehn-fehr-meh-DAHD dehl EE-gah-thoh
lobster	*langosta*	lahn-GOH-stah
loose stools	*excrementos sueltos*	ehk-skreh-MEHN-tohs SWEHL-tohs
	heces sueltas	EH-sehs SWEHL-tahs
low blood pressure	*presión (arterial) baja*	preh-see-OHN (ahr-teh-ree-AHL) BAH-hah
	baja presión	BAH-hah preh-see-OHN
low-fat	*bajo/a en grasa*	BAH-hoh/hah ehn GRAH-sah
low-fat milk	*leche de un porciento*	LEH-cheh deh oon pohr-see-EHN-toh
	leche descremada	LEH-cheh dehs-kreh-MAH-thah
low-salt	*bajo en sal*	BAH-hoh ehn sahl
low-sodium	*bajo en sodio*	BAH-hoh ehn SOH-thee-oh
	reducido en sodio	rreh-thoo-SEE-thoh ehn SOH-thee-oh
lunch	*almuerzo*	ahl-MWEHR-soh
	comida	koh-MEE-thah
	lonche	LOHN-cheh

M

magnesium	*magnesio*	mahg-NEH-see-oh
main dish	*plato principal*	PLAH-toh preen-see-PAHL
malnutrition	*desnutrición*	dehs-noo-tree-see-OHN
mango	*mango*	MAHN-goh
margarine	*margarina*	mahr-gah-REE-nah
	aceite vegetal hidrogenado	ah-SEH-ee-teh beh-heh-TAHL ee-droh-heh-NAH-thoh
mayonnaise	*mayonesa*	mah-yoh-NEE-sah
meatballs	*albóndigas*	ahl-BOHN-dee-gahs
melt	*derretir*	deh-rreh-TEER
microwaved	*cocido/a en microondas*	koh-SEE-thoh/thah ehn mee-kroh-OHN dahs
milk	*leche*	LEH-cheh
milkshake	*batido*	bah-TEE-thoh
	licuado	lee-KWAH-thoh
mineral water	*agua mineral*	AH-gwah mee-neh-RAHL
minerals	*minerales*	mee-neh-RAH-lehs
Miss	*Señorita*	sehn-yoh-REE-tah

mix	*mezclar*	mehs-KLAHR
(in) moderation	*(con) moderación*	(kohn) moh-deh-rah-see-OHN
Monday	*lunes*	LOOH-nehs
monounsaturated fat	*grasa monoinsaturada*	GRAH-sah moh-noh-een-sah-tuh-RAH-thah
Monterey Jack cheese	*queso monterey jack*	KEH soh Kmohn-teh-reh JAHK
more	*más*	mahs
mozzarella cheese	*queso mozzarella*	KEH-soh moht-seh-REH-lah
Mr.	*Señor*	sehn-YOHR
Mrs.	*Señora*	sehn-YOH-rah
Ms.	*Señorita*	sehn-yoh-REE-tah
muffin	*panque*	PAHN-keh
	panecillo	pah-neh-SEE-yoh
	mollete	moh-YEH-teh
	muffin	MOH-feen
mushroom	*hongo*	OHN-goh
	champiñon	chahm-peen-YOHN
mustard	*mostaza*	moh-STAH-sah

N

nausea	*nauseas*	NOW-see-ahs
nectarine	*nectarina*	nehk-tah-REE-nah
	pelón	peh-LOHN
never	*nunca*	NOON-kah
nonfat (skim) milk	*leche sin grasa*	LEH-cheh seen GRAH-sah
	leche desgrasada	LEH-cheh-dehs-grah-SAH-thah
	leche descremada	LEH-cheh dehs-kreh-MAH-thah
noodles (thin pasta, vermicelli)	*fideos*	fee-THEH-yohs
normally	*normalmente*	nohr-mahl-MEHN-teh
nutmeg	*nuez moscada*	noo-EHS mohs-KAH-thah
nutritious	*nutritivo/a*	noo-tree-tee-boh/bah
nuts	*nueces*	noo-EH-sehs
	frutos secos	FROO-tohs SEH-kohs

O

oatmeal	*avena*	ah-BEH-nah
oats	*avena*	ah-BEH-nah
obesity	*obesidad*	oh-beh-see-DAHD
	gordura	gohr-DOO-rah
octopus	*pulpo*	POOL-poh
oil	*aceite*	ah-SEH-ee-teh
okra	*quingombó*	keen-gohm-BOH
	calabú	kah-lah-BOO
	quimbombó	keem-bohm-BOH
olive oil	*aceite de oliva*	ah-SEH-ee-teh deh oh-LEE-bah
onion	*cebolla*	seh-BOH-yah
orange	*naranja*	nah-RAHN-hah
	china	CHEE-nah
orange juice	*jugo de naranja*	HOO-goh deh nah-RAHN-hah
	jugo de china	HOO-goh deh CHEE-nah
oregano	*orégano*	oh-REH-gah-noh
ounce(s)	*onza(s)*	OHN-sah(s)

| overweight | *sobrepeso* | soh-breh-PEH-soh |
| oysters | *ostiones* | oh-stee-OH-nehs |

P

pancakes	*panqueques*	pahn-KEH-kehs
	panques	PAHN-kehs
	crepas	KREH-pahs
	panquecas	pahn-KEH-kahs
	hotcakes	HOHT-kehks
pancreas	*páncreas*	PAHN-kreh-ahs
papaya	*papaya*	pah-PAH-yah
	fruta bomba	FROO-tah BOHM-bah
parsley	*perejil*	peh-reh-HEEL
passion fruit	*granadilla*	grah-nah-DEE-yah
	maracuyá	mah-rah-koo-YAH
	parcha	PAHR-chah
paste (sauce)	*mole*	MOH-leh
	salsa	SAHL-sah
pastry	*pan dulce*	pahn DOOL-seh

peach	*durazno*	doo-RAHS-noh
	melocotón	meh-loh-koh-TOHN
peanut butter	*crema de cacahuate*	KREH-mah deh kah-kah-WAH-the
	crema de maní	KREH-mah deh mah-NEE
	mantequilla de cacahuate	mahn-teh-KEE-ya deh kah-kah-WAH-teh
	mantequilla de maní	mahn-teh-KEE-ya deh mah-NEE
	manteca de maní	mahn-TEH-kah deh mah-NEE
peanuts	*cacahuates*	kah-kah-WAH-tehs
	maníes	mah-NEE-yehs
pear	*pera*	PEH-rah
pecans	*pacanas*	pah-KAH-nahs
	nueces	noo-EH-sehs
peel (off)	*pelar*	peh-LAHR
pepper (black)	*pimienta negra*	pee-mee-YEHN-tah NEH-grah
pepper (white)	*pimienta blanca*	pee-mee-YEHN-tah BLAHN-kah

peppers, stuffed	*chiles rellenos*	CHEE-lehs rreh-YEH-nohs
	ajíes rellenos	ah-HEE-yehs rreh-YEH-nohs
	pimientos rellenos	pee-mee-YEHN-tohs rreh-YEH-nohs
percent	*porciento*	pohr-see-EHN-toh
percentage	*porcentaje*	pohr-sehn-TAH-heh
phosphorus	*fósforo*	FOHS-foh-roh
pickled	*en vinagre*	ehn vee-NAH-greh
pie	*pai*	PAH-ee
	pastel	pah-STEHL
	empanada	ehm-pah-NAH-thah
	tarta	TAHR-tah
	torta	TOHR-tah
piece(s)	*trozo(s)*	TROH-soh(s)
	pedazo(s)	peh-THAH-soh(s)
pine nuts	*piñones*	peen-YOH-nehs
pineapple	*piña*	PEEN-yah
	ananá	ah-nah-NAH
pizza	*pizza*	PEET-sah

plantain	*plátano*	PLAH-tah-noh
	plátano macho	PLAH-tah-noh MAH-choh
	plátano grande	PLAH-tah-noh GRAHN-deh
plum	*ciruela*	seer-WEH-lah
polyunsatu-rated fat	*grasa poliinsaturada*	GRAH-sah poh-lee-een-sah-tuh-RAH-thah
pomegranate	*granada*	grah-NAH-thah
popcorn	*palomitas (de maíz)*	pah-loh-MEE-tahs (deh mah-EES)
pork	*puerco*	PWEHR-koh
	cerdo	SEHR-thoh
pork chop	*chuleta de puerco*	choo-LEH-tah deh PWEHR-koh
	chuleta de cerdo	choo-LEH-tah deh SEHR-thoh
	costilla de cerolo	koh-STEE-yah deh seh-ROH-loh
	costilla de cerdo	koh-STEE-yah deh SEHR-thoh
pork skins, fried	*chicharrones*	chee-cha-RROH-nehs

portion	*porción*	pohr-see-OHN
	racion	rah-see-OHN
potassium	*potasio*	poh-TAH-see-oh
potatoes	*papas*	PAH-pahs
	patatas	pah-TAH-tahs
powdered milk	*leche en polvo*	LEH-cheh ehn POHL-boh
prepared	*preparado/a*	preh-pah-RAH-thoh/thah
pretzel	*prétzel*	PREHT-sehl
protein	*proteína*	proh-teh-EE-nah
prunes	*ciruelas pasas*	seer-WEH-lahs PAH-sahs
	pasas	PAH-sahs
	pasas de uva	PAH-sahs deh OO-bah
pudding	*pudin*	poo-THEEN
pumpkin	*calabaza*	cah-lah-BAH-sah
pumpkin seeds	*pepitas*	peh-PEE-tahs

Q

| quinoa | *quínoa* | KEEN-wah |

R

radish	*rábano*	RRAH-bah-noh
raisins	*uvas pasas*	OO-bahs PAH-sahs
raspberries	*frambuesas*	frahm-BWEH-sahs
raw	*crudo/a*	KROO-thoh/thah
red wine	*vino tinto*	BEE-noh TEEN-toh
	vino rojo	BEE-noh RROH-hoh
reduced-fat (2%) milk	*leche de dos porciento*	LEH-cheh deh dohs pohr-see-EHN-toh
refried beans	*frijoles refritos*	free-HOH-lehs rreh-FREE-tohs
renal disease	*enfermedad renal*	ehn-fehr-meh-DAHD rreh-NAHL
	enfermedad de los riñones	ehn-fehr-meh-DAHD deh lohs rreen-YOH-nehs
rice	*arroz*	ah-RROHS
rinse (off)	*enjuagar*	ehn-hwah-GAHR
rolled	*enrollado*	ehn-roh-YAH-thoh

S

salad	*ensalada*	ehn-sah-LAH-thah
salad dressing	*aderezo*	ah-deh-REH-soh
	aliño	ah-LEEN-yoh
	condimento	kohn-dee-MEHN-toh
salt	*sal*	sahl
salt-free	*sin sal*	seen sahl
saltines	*galletas saladas*	gah-YEH-tahs sah-LAH-thahs
	galletitas de agua	gah-yeh-TEE-tahs deh AH-gwah
sandwich	*sándwich*	SAHND-weech
	torta	TOHR-tah
	bocadillo	boh-kah-DEE-yoh
	emparedado	ehm-pah-reh-THAH-thoh
saturated fat	*grasa saturada*	GRAH-sah sah-too-RAH-thah
Saturday	*sábado*	SAH-bah-thoh
sauce	*mole*	MOH-leh
	salsa	SAHL-sah

sausage	*salchicha*	sahl-CHEE-chah
	chorizo	choh-REE-soh
sautéed	*sofrito/a*	soh-FREE-toh/thah
	salteado/a	sahl-teh-AH-thoh/thah
selenium	*selenio*	seh-LEH-nee-oh
served	*servido/a*	sehr-BEE-thoh/thah
serving size	*porciónes*	pohr-see-OH-nehs
	raciones	rah-see-OH-nehs
shallots	*chalotes*	chah-LOH-tehs
	chalotas	chah-LOH-tahs
shaved ice, with flavored syrup	*raspado*	rrah-SPAH-thoh
	piraguas	pee-RAH-gwahs
shellfish	*mariscos*	mah-REE-skohs
sherbet/ sorbet	*sorbete*	sohr-BEH-teh
	helado de nieve	eh-LAH-thoh deh nee-eh-beh
	helado de agua	eh-LAH-thoh deh AH-gwah
shrimp	*camarón*	kah-mah-ROHN
skim	*descremado/a*	dehs-kreh-MAH-thoh/thah
skirt steak	*fajita*	fah-HEE-tah

slice	*rebanada*	rreh-bah-NAH-thah
	rodaja	rroh-DAH-hah
	feta	FEH-tah
sliced	*rebanado/a*	rreh-bah-NAH-thoh/thah
	tajado/a	tah-HAH-thoh/thah
small piece(s)	*trocito(s)*	troh-SEE-toh(s)
	pedacito(s)	peh-thah-SEE-toh(s)
snack	*merienda*	meh-ree-EHN-dah
	bocadillo	boh-kah-DEE-yoh
	entrecomidas	ehn-treh-koh-MEE-thahs
sodium	*sodio*	SOH-thee-oh
soft drink	*refresco*	rreh-FREHS-koh
	gaseosa	gah-seh-OH-sah
	soda	SOH-thah
soup	*sopa*	SOH-pah
	caldo	KAHL-doh
soybean oil	*aceite de soya*	ah-SEH-ee-teh deh SOH-yah
spaghetti	*espaguetis*	eh-spah-GEH-tees

sparkling water	*agua con gas*	AH-gwah kohn GAHS
	agua gasificada	AH-gwah gah-see-fee-KAH-thah
	agua mineral	AH-gwah mee-neh-RAHL
spices	*especias*	ehs-PEH-see-ahs
spinach	*espinacas*	eh-spee-NAH-kahs
spread	*untado/a*	oon-TAH-thoh/thah
squid	*calamar*	kah-lah-MAHR
steak	*bistec*	BEE-stehk or bee-STEHK
	bife	BEE-feh
	guisado	ghee-SAH-thoh
steamed	*cocido/a al vapor*	koh-SEE-thoh/thah ahl bah-POHR
	al vapor	ahl bah-POHR
stewed	*guisado/a*	ghee-SAH-thoh/ah
stir-fried	*sofrito/a*	soh-FREE-toh/tah
	salteado/a	sahl-teh-AH-thoh/thah
strain	*escurrir*	ehs-koo-RREER
strawberries	*fresas*	FREH-sahs
	frutillas	froo-TEE-yahs

strip(s)	*tira(s)*	TEE-rah(s)
stuffed	*relleno/a*	rreh-YEH-noh/nah
sugar	*azúcar*	ah-SOO-kahr
sugar, brown or light brown	*azúcar rubia*	ah-SOO-kahr RROO-bee-yah
	azúcar morena	ah-SOO-kahr moh-REH-nah
sugar, dark brown, unrefined	*piloncillo*	pee-lohn-SEE-yoh
	azúcar negra	ah-SOO-kahr NEH-grah
sugar-free	*sin azúcar*	seen ah-SOO-kahr
Sunday	*domingo*	doh-MEEN-goh
sweet potatoes	*batatas*	bah-TAH-tahs
	camotes	kah-MOH-tehs
	boniatos	boh-nee-YAH-tohs
sweetbreads	*mollejas*	moh-YEH-hahs
sweetened condensed milk	*leche condensada*	LEH-cheh kohn-dehn-SAH-thah
sweets	*dulces*	DOOL-sehs
	caramelos	kah-rah-MEH-lohs
	golosinas	goh-loh-SEE-nahs

swiss cheese	*queso suizo*	KEH-soh SWEE-soh
syrup	*almíbar*	ahl-MEE-bahr
	sirope	see-ROH-peh
	jarabe	ha-RAH-beh

T

tablespoon	*cucharada*	koo-chah-RAH-thah
tangerine	*mandarina*	mahn-dah-REE-nah
tea	*té*	teh
teaspoon	*cucharadita*	koo-chah-rah-THEE-tah
	cucharadita tipo/ de té	koo-chah-rah-TEEH-tah tee-poh/theh TEH
test strip	*tira de ensayo*	TEE-rah deh ehn-SAH-yoh
thirst	*sed*	sehd
Thursday	*jueves*	HWEH-behs
tired	*sueño*	SWEHN-yoh
toast	*pan tostado*	pahn toh-STAH-thoh
	tostadas	tohs-TAH-thahs
tomatillo	*tomatillo*	toh-mah-TEE-yoh

tomato	*tomate*	toh-MAH-teh
	jitomate	hee-toh-MAH-teh
tomato juice	*jugo de tomate*	HOO-goh deh toh-MAH-teh
	jugo de jitomate	HOO-go deh hee-toh-MAH-teh
too much	*demasiado/a*	deh-mah-see-AH-thoh/thah
	excesivo/a	ehk-seh-SEE-boh/bah
tortilla	*tortilla*	tohr-TEE-yah
tripe	*tripas*	TREE-pahs
Tuesday	*martes*	MAHR-tehs
tuna	*atún*	ah-TOON
turkey	*pavo*	PAH-boh
	guajolote	gwah-hoh-LOH-teh
turnip	*nabo*	NAH-boh

U

unsaturated fat	*grasa no saturada*	GRAH-sah no sah-too-RAH-thah
	grasa insaturada	GRAH-sah een-sah-too-RAH-thah

urine	*orina*	oh-REE-nah
	pipi (informal)	PEE-pee
	chi (informal)	chee
usually	*usualmente*	oo-soo-ahl-MEHN-teh

V

vegetable juice	*jugo de vegetales*	HOO-goh deh beh-heh-TAH-lehs
	jugo de verduras	HOO-goh deh behr-DOO-rahs
	v ocho	beh-oh-choh
very	*muy*	moo-wee
vitamin(s)	*vitamina(s)*	bee-tah-MEE-nah(s)
vomit	*vómito(s)*	BOH-mee-toh(s)

W

waffles	*wafles*	WAH-flehs
walnuts	*nueces de Castilla*	noo-EH-sehs deh kahs-TEE-yah
	nueces	noo-EH-sehs
	nueces de nogal	noo-EH-sehs deh noh-GAHL

water	*agua*	AH-gwah
watermelon	*sandía*	sahn-DEE-yah
	patilla	pah-TEE-yah
Wednesday	*miércoles*	mee-YEHR-koh-lehs
well	*bien*	bee-EHN
well-done	*bien hecho/a*	bee-ehn EH-choh/chah
	bien cocido/a	bee-ehn koh-SEE-thoh/thah
wheat bread	*pan de trigo*	pahn deh TREE-goh
wheat flour	*harina de trigo*	ah-REE-nah deh TREE-goh
wheat toast	*pan de trigo tostado*	pahn deh TREE-go toh-STAH-thoh
when	*cúando*	KWAHN-doh
whiskey	*whiskey*/güisqui	WEES-kee
white bread	*pan blanco*	pahn BLAHN-koh
white cheese	*queso blanco*	KEH-soh BLAHN-koh
white cheese made with cow's milk	*queso asadero*	KEH-soh ah-sah-DEH-roh
	chihuahua	chee-WAH-wah
	oaxaca	wah-HAH-kah
	queso fresco	KEH-soh FREHS-koh
white rice	*arroz blanco*	ah-RROHS BLAHN-koh

white toast	*pan blanco tostado*	pahn BLAHN-koh toh-STAH-thoh
white wine	*vino blanco*	BEE-noh BLAHN-koh
whole grain	*integral*	een-teh-GRAHL
whole grain bread	*pan integral*	pahn een-teh-GRAHL
whole grain flour	*harina (de trigo) integral*	ah-REE-nah (deh TREE-goh) een-teh-GRAHL
whole grain toast	*pan integral tostado*	pahn een-teh-GRAHL toh-STAH-thoh
whole milk	*leche entera*	LEH-cheh ehn-TEH-rah
	leche sin descremar	LEH-cheh seen dehs-kreh-MAHR
whole wheat	*de trigo integral*	deh TREE-goh een-teh-GRAHL
wild rice	*arroz silvestre*	ah-RROHS seel-BEHS-treh
	arroz salvaje	ah-RROHS sahl-BAH-heh
wine	*vino*	BEE-noh
with	*con*	kohn
with less salt	*con menos sal*	kohn MEH-nohs sahl
without	*sin*	seen

Y

| yogurt | *yogur* | yoh-GOOR |

Z

zucchini	*calabacita*	kah-lah-bah-SEE-tah
	calabacín	kah-lah-bah-SEEN
	zapallito	sah-pah-YEE-toh

Spanish to English Glossary

Some Spanish adjectives can end in either the letter "o" or "a," depending on the gender of the noun that the adjective modifies. These are represented in this appendix with a slash between the oh and ah sound. For example:

| boiled | *hervido/a* | ehr-BEE-thoh/thah |

See chapter 7 for more details.

Numeros

cero	SEH-roh	zero
uno	OO-noh	one
dos	dohs	two

tres	trehs	three
cuatro	KWAH-troh	four
cinco	SEEN-koh	five
seis	SEH-ees	six
siete	see-EH-teh	seven
ocho	OH-choh	eight
nueve	noo-EH-beh	nine
diez	dee-ehs	ten
once	OHN-seh	eleven
doce	DOH-seh	twelve
trece	TREH-seh	thirteen
catorce	kah-TOHR-seh	fourteen
quince	KEEN-seh	fifteen
veinte	BEHN-teh	twenty
treinta	TREHN-tah	thirty
cuarenta	kwah-REHN-tah	forty
cincuenta	seen-KWEHN-tah	fifty
sesenta	seh-SEHN-tah	sixty
setenta	seh-TEHN-tah	seventy
ochenta	oh-CHEHN-tah	eighty

noventa	noh-BEHN-tah	ninety
cien	see-EHN	one hundred
ciento	see-EHN-toh	
doscientos	dohs-see-EHN-tohs	two hundred
trescientos	trehs-see-EHN-tohs	three hundred
cuatrocientos	kwah-troh-see-EHN-tohs	four hundred
quinientos	kee-nee-YEHN-tohs	five hundred
seiscientos	see-ehs-see-EHN-tohs	six hundred
setecientos	seh-teh-see-EHN-tohs	seven hundred
ochocientos	oh-choh-see-EHN-tohs	eight hundred
novecientos	noh-beh-see-EHN-tohs	nine hundred
mil	meel	one thousand
dos mil	dohs meel	two thousand
tres mil	trehs meel	three thousand

A

a la parrilla	ah lah pah-RREE-yah	broiled
aceite	ah-SEH-ee-teh	oil
aceite de canola	ah-SEH-ee-teh deh kah-NOH-lah	canola oil

aceite de maíz	ah-SEH-ee-teh deh mah-EES	corn oil
aceite de oliva	ah-SEH-ee-teh deh oh-LEE-bah	olive oil
aceite de soya	ah-SEH-ee-teh deh SOH-yah	soybean oil
aceite vegetal hidrogenado	ah-SEH-ee-teh beh-heh-TAHL ee-droh-heh-NAH-thoh	margarine
achiote	ah-chee-YOH-teh	achiote (seasoning paste made from annatto seeds)
acidéz	ah-see-THEHS	heartburn acid reflux
ácido fólico	AH-see-thoh FOH-lee-koh	folic acid
aderezo	ah-deh-REH-soh	salad dressing
agua	AH-gwah	water
agua con gas	AH-gwah kohn GAHS	sparkling water
agua de sabor	AH-gwah deh sah-BOR	flavored water

agua gasificada	AH-gwah gah-see-fee-KAH-thah	sparkling water
agua mineral	AH-gwah mee-neh-RAHL	mineral water
		sparkling water
agua saborizada	AH-gwah sah-boh-ree-SAH-thah	flavored water
aguacate	ah-gwah-KAH-teh	avocado
aji verde	ah-HEE BEHR-deh	green bell pepper
ajíes rellenos	ah-HEE-yehs rreh-YEH-nohs	peppers, stuffed
ajo	AH-hoh	garlic
al carbón	ahl kahr-BOHN	barbecued meat
al horno	ahl OHR-noh	baked
al vapor	ahl bah-POHR	steamed
albaricoque	ahl-bah-ree-KOH-keh	apricot
albóndigas	ahl-BOHN-dee-gahs	meatballs
alergia al gluten	ah-LEHR-hee-ah ahl GLOO-tehn	gluten allergy

aliño	ah-LEEN-yoh	salad dressing
almejas	ahl-MEH-hahs	clams
almendras	ahl-MEHN-drahs	almonds
almíbar	ahl-MEE-bahr	syrup
almuerzo	ahl-MWEHR-soh	lunch
alta presión	AHL-tah preh-see-OHN	high blood pressure
anacardos	ah-nah-KAHR-thos	cashews
ananá	ah-nah-NAH	pineapple
anemia	ah-NEH-mee-ah	anemia
anoréxico/a	ah-noh-REK-see-koh/kah	anorexic
antojito	ahn-toh-HEE-toh	appetizer
aperitivo	ah-peh-ree-TEE-boh	appetizer
apio	AH-pee-oh	celery
aproximadamente	ah-PROHK-see-mah-thah MEHN-teh	approximately
arándanos (azules)	ah-RAHN-dah-nohs (ah-SOO-lehs)	blueberries
arándanos rojos (y agrios)	ah-RAHN-dah-nohs RROH-hohs (ee AH-gree-ohs)	cranberries

arroz	ah-RROHS	rice
arroz blanco	ah-RROHS BLAHN-koh	white rice
arroz integral	ah-RROHS een-teh-GRAHL	brown rice
arroz moreno	ah-RROHS moh-REH-noh	brown rice
arroz salvaje	ah-RROHS sahl-BAH-heh	wild rice
arroz silvestre	ah-RROHS seel-BEHS-treh	wild rice
asado/a	ah-SAH-thoh/thah	grilled
ate	AH-the	jelly
atún	ah-TOON	tuna
avellanas	ah-beh-YEHN-ahs	hazelnuts
avena	ah-BEH-nah	oatmeal
		oats
azúcar	ah-SOO-kahr	sugar
azúcar morena	ah-SOO-kahr moh-REH-nah	sugar, brown or light brown
azúcar negra	ah-SOO-kahr NEH-grah	sugar, dark brown, unrefined
azúcar rubia	ah-SOO-kahr RROO-bee-yah	sugar, brown or light brown
azúcares	ah-SOO-kah-rehs	sugar

B

bajo/a presión	BAH-hah preh-see-OHN	low blood pressure
bajo/a en grasa	BAH-hoh/hah ehn GRAH-sah	low-fat
bajo/a en sal	BAH-hoh/hah ehn sahl	low-salt
bajo/a en sodio	BAH-hoh/hah ehn SOH-thee-oh	low-sodium
banana/banano	bah-NAH-nah	banana
barbacoa	bahr-bah-KOH-ah	barbecued meat
batatas	bah-TAH-tahs	sweet potatoes
batido	bah-TEE-thoh	milkshake
bebida	beh-BEE-thah	beverage
		drink
berenjena	beh-rehn-HEH-nah	eggplant
betabel	beh-tah-BEHL	beet
bien	bee-EHN	fine
		well
bien cocido/a	bee-ehn koh-SEE-thoh/thah	well-done
bien hecho/a	bee-ehn EH-choh/chah	well-done

bife	BEE-feh	steak
bistec	BEE-stehk or bee-STEHK	steak
bizcochito	bees-koh-CHEE-toh	cupcake
bizcocho	bees-KOH-choh	cake
blanquear	blahn-keh-AHR	blanch
blanquillos	blahn-KEE-yohs	eggs
bocadillo	boh-kah-DEE-yoh	sandwich
		snack
bolillo	boh-LEE-yoh	bread roll
boniatos	boh-nee-YAH-tohs	sweet potatoes
brécol	BREH-kohl	broccoli
broccoli	BROH-koh-lee	broccoli
bruselas	broo-SEH-lahs	brussels sprouts
bulímico/a	boo-LEE-mee-koh/kah	bulimic

C

caca	KAH-kah	feces (informal)
cacahuates	kah-kah-WAH-tehs	peanuts
café	kah-FEH	coffee

café con leche	kah-FEH kohn LEH-cheh	coffee with milk and sugar
calabacín/ calabacita	kah-lah-bah-SEEN	zucchini
	kah-lah-bah-SEE-tah	zucchini
calabaza	cah-lah-BAH-sah	pumpkin
calabú	kah-lah-BOO	okra
calamar	kah-lah-MAHR	squid
caldo	KAHL-doh	soup
caliente	kah-lee-EHN-teh	hot (temperature)
caloría(s)	kah-loh-REE-ah(s)	calorie(s)
alostro	cah-LOH-stroh	colostrum
camarón	kah-mah-ROHN	shrimp
camotes	kah-MOH-tehs	sweet potatoes
canela	kah-NEH-lah	cinnamon
cantalupo	kahn-tah-LOO-poh	cantaloupe
caramelos	kah-rah-MEH-lohs	candy
		sweets
carbohidrato(s)	kahr-boh-ee-DRAH-toh(s)	carbohydrate(s)
carne a la plancha	KAHR-neh ah lah PLAHN-chah	grilled beef

carne a la tampiqueña	KAHR-neh ah lah tahm-pee-KEHN-yah	grilled beef
carne asada	KAHR-neh ah-SAH-thah	grilled beef
carne de res	KAHR-neh deh RREHS	beef
carne molida	KAHR-neh moh-LEE-thah	ground beef
carne para sándwich	KAHR-neh pah-rah SAHND-weech	cold cuts
carne picada	KAHR-neh pee-KAH-thah	ground beef
carne roja	KAHR-neh RROH-hah	beef
carnero	kahr-NEH-roh	lamb
castaña de cajú	kahs-TAHN-yah deh kah-HOO	cashews
catorce	kah-TOHR-seh	fourteen
catsup	KAHT-soop	ketchup
cebada	seh-BAH-thah	barley
cebolla	seh-BOH-yah	onion
cebolla de verdeo	seh-BOH-yah theh behr-THEH-oh	green onion/ scallion
cebolla larga	seh-BOH-yah LAHR-gah	green onion/ scallion
cebolleta	seh-BOH-YEH-tah	green onion/ scallion
cena	SEH-nah	dinner

cerdo	SEHR-thoh	pork
cereal	seh-reh-AHL	cereal
cerezas	seh-REH-sahs	cherries
cero	SEH-roh	zero
cerveza	sehr-BEH-sah	beer
chabacano	chah-bah-KAH-noh	apricot
chalotas	chah-LOH-tahs	shallots
chalotes	chah-LOH-tehs	shallots
champiñon	chahm-peen-YOHN	mushroom
chi	chee	urine (informal)
chícharos	CHEE-chah-rohs	green peas
chicharrones	chee-cha-RROH-nehs	pork skins, fried
chihuahua	chee-WAH-wah	white cheese made with cow's milk
chile	CHEE-leh	chili pepper
chile ancho	CHEE-leh AHN-choh	green bell pepper
chile con carne	CHEE-leh kohn KAHR-neh	chili with meat
chile en polvo	CHEE-leh ehn POHL-boh	chili powder (contains garlic and cumin)

chile verde	CHEE-leh BEHR-deh	green bell pepper
chiles rellenos	CHEE-lehs rreh-YEH-nohs	peppers, stuffed
china	CHEE-nah	orange
chips	cheeps	chips (snack chips)
choclo de maíz	CHOH-kloh deh mah-EES	corn on the cob
chocolate	choh-koh-LAH-teh	chocolate
		hot chocolate
chorizo	choh-REE-soh	sausage
chuleta de cerdo	choo-LEH-tah deh SEHR-thoh	pork chop
chuleta de puerco	choo-LEH-tah deh PWEHR-koh	pork chop
cien	see-EHN	one hundred
ciento	see-EHN-toh	one hundred
cilandro/cilantro	see-LAHND-roh	cilantro
		coriander
cinco	SEEN-koh	five
cincuenta	seen-KWEHN-tah	fifty

ciruela	seer-WEH-lah	plum
ciruelas pasas	seer-WEH-lahs PAH-sahs	prunes
clara de blanquillo	KLAH-rah deh blahn-KEE-yoh	egg white
clara de huevo	KLAH-rah deh WEH-boh	egg white
cocido/a en microondas	koh-SEE-thoh/thah ehn mee-kroh-OHN dahs	microwaved
cocido/a al vapor	koh-SEE-thoh/thah ahl bah-POHR	steamed
coco	KOH-koh	coconut
col	kohl	cabbage
col de Bruselas	kohl deh broo-SEH-lahs	brussels sprouts
colecitas de Bruselas	koh-leh-SEE-tahs deh broo-SEH-lahs	brussels sprouts
colesterol	koh-lehs-teh-ROHL	cholesterol
colesterol alto	koh-lehs-teh-ROHL AHL-toh	high cholesterol
coliflor	koh-lee-FLOHR	cauliflower
comida	koh-MEE-thah	lunch
comino	koh-MEE-noh	cumin
con	kohn	with

con menos sal	kohn MEH-nohs sahl	with less salt
condimento	kohn-dee-MEHN-toh	salad dressing
congelado/a	kohn-heh-LAH-thoh/thah	frozen
constipación	kohn-stee-pah-see-OHN	constipation
corazón	koh-rah-SOHN	heart
cordero	kohr-THEH-roh	lamb
coriandro	koh-ree-AHN-droh	cilantro
		coriander
cortado/a	kohr-TAH-thoh/thah	cut up
costilla de cerdo	koh-STEE-yah deh SEHR-thoh	pork chop
costilla de cerolo	koh-STEE-yah deh seh-ROH-loh	pork chop
crema	KREH-mah	cream
crema de cacahuate	KREH-mah deh kah-kah-WAH-teh	peanut butter
crema de maní	KREH-mah deh mah-NEE	peanut butter
crepas	KREH-pahs	pancakes
crudo/a	KROO-thoh/thah	raw
cúando	KWAHN-doh	when
cuántos/as	KWAHN-tohs/tahs	how many

cuarenta	kwah-REHN-tah	forty
cuatro	KWAH-troh	four
cuatrocientos	kwah-troh-see-EHN-tohs	four hundred
cubilete	koo-bee-LEH-teh	cupcake
cubitos	koo-BEE-tohs	cube(s)
cubo(s)	KOO-boh(s)	cube(s)
cucharada	koo-chah-RAH-thah	tablespoon
cucharadita	koo-chah-rah-THEE-tah	teaspoon
cucharadita tipo de té	koo-chah-rah-TEEH-tah tee-poh deh TEH	teaspoon
culantro	koo-LAHN-troh	cilantro
		coriander

D

damasco	dah-MAHS-koh	apricot
dátil	DAH-teel	date
de trigo integral	deh TREE-goh een-teh-GRAHL	whole wheat
demasiado/a	deh-mah-see-AH-thoh/ thah	too much
derretir	deh-rreh-TEER	melt

desayuno	deh-sah-YOO-noh	breakfast
descremado/a	dehs-kreh-MAH-thoh/thah	skim
deshuesar	dehs-weh-SAHR	devein
		debone
desnutrición	dehs-noo-tree-see-OHN	malnutrition
diabetes	dee-ah-BEH-tehs	diabetes
diabetes del embarazo	dee-ah-BEH-tehs dehl ehm-bah-RAH-soh	gestational diabetes
diabetes gestacional	dee-ah-BEH-tehs hehs-tah-see-oh-NAHL	gestational diabetes
diarrea	dee-ah-RREH-ah	diarrhea
diente de ajo	dee-EHN-teh deh AH-hoh	garlic clove
dieta	dee-EH-tah	diet
diez	dee-ehs	ten
doce	DOH-she	twelve
dolores de cabeza	doh-LOH-rehs deh kah-BEH-sah	headaches
domingo	doh-MEEN-goh	Sunday
donas	DOH-nahs	donuts
dos	dohs	two
dos mil	dohs meel	two thousand

doscientos	dohs-see-EHN-tohs	two hundred
dulce	DOOL-seh	jelly
dulces	DOOL-sehs	candy
		cookies
		sweets
durazno	doo-RAHS-noh	peach

E

ejotes	eh-HOH-tehs	green beans
elote	eh-LOH-teh	corn
		corn on the cob
embutidos	ehm-boo-TEE-thohs	cold cuts
empanada	ehm-pah-NAH-thah	pie
emparedado	ehm-pah-reh-THAH-thoh	sandwich
en lata	ehn LAH-tah	canned
en vinagre	ehn vee-NAH-greh	pickled
endulzante (artificial)	ehn-dool-SAHN-teh (ahr-tee-fee-see-AHL)	artificial sweetener
energía	eh-nehr-HEE-ah	energy
enfermedad	ehn-fehr-meh-DAHD	disease

enfermedad de los riñones	ehn-fehr-meh-DAHD deh lohs reen-YOH-nehs	renal disease
enfermedad del hígado	ehn-fehr-meh-DAHD dehl EE-gah-thoh	liver disease
enfermedad renal	ehn-fehr-meh-DAHD reh-NAHL	renal disease
enjuagar	ehn-hwah-GAHR	rinse (off)
enlatado/a	ehn-lah-TAH-thoh/thah	canned
enrollado	ehn-roh-YAH-thoh	rolled
ensalada	ehn-sah-LAH-thah	salad
ensalada de col	ehn-sah-LAH-thah deh KOHL	cole slaw
ensalada de repollo	ehn-sah-LAH-thah deh rreh-POH-yoh	cole slaw
entrada	ehn-TRAH-thah	appetizer
entrecomidas	ehn-treh-koh-MEE-thahs	snack
escaldar	ehs-kahl-DAHR	blanch
escurrir	ehs-koo-RREER	strain
espaguetis/ espaguettis	eh-spah-GEH-tees	spaghetti
especias	ehs-PEH-see-ahs	spices

espinaca	eh-spee-NAH-kah	spinach
estofar	eh-stoh-FAHR	braise
estreñimiento	ehs-trehn-yee-mee-EHN-toh	constipation
etiqueta	eh-tee-KEH-tah	label
excesivo/a	ehk-seh-SEE-boh/bah	too much
excremento	eks-kreh-MEHN-toh	bowel movement
		feces
excrementos sueltos	ehk-skreh-MEHN-tohs SWEHL-tohs	loose stools
extractor de leche materna	ehk-strahk-TOHR deh LEH-cheh mah-TERN-nah	breast pump

F

fajita	fah-HEE-tah	skirt steak
feta	FEH-tah	slice
fibra	FEE-brah	fiber
fideos	fee-THEH-yohs	noodles (thin pasta, vermicelli)
flan	flahn	custard

fósforo	FOHS-foh-roh	phosphorus
flatulencia	flah-too-LEHN-see-ah	flatulance
		gas
frambuesas	frahm-BWEH-sahs	raspberries
fresas	FREH-sahs	strawberries
fresco/a	FREHS-koh/kah	fresh
frijoles	free-HOH-lehs	beans
frijoles refritos	free-HOH-lehs rreh-FREE-tohs	refried beans
frío/a	free-oh/free-ah	cooked
frito/a	FREE-toh/tah	fried
fruta bomba	FROO-tah BOHM-bah	papaya
frutas	FROO-tahs	fruits
frutillas	froo-TEE-yahs	strawberries
frutos secos	FROO-tohs SEH-kohs	nuts

G

galletas	gah-YEH-tahs	cookies
galletas saladas	gah-YEH-tahs sah-LAH-thahs	saltines/ crackers

galletitas de agua	gah-yeh-TEE-tahs deh AH-gwah	saltines/crackers
gaseosa	gah-seh-OH-sah	soft drink
gaseosa de dieta	gah-seh-OH-sah deh dee-EH-tah	diet soft drink
gaseosa lite	gah-seh-OH-sah LAHYT	diet soft drink
gases	GAH-sehs	gas
		flatulence
gelatina	heh-lah-TEE-nah	gelatin
generalmente	heh-neh-rahl-MEHN-teh	generally
golosinas	goh-loh-SEE-nahs	candy
		sweets
gordura	gohr-DOO-rah	obesity
gramo(s)	GRAH-moh(s)	gram(s)
granada	grah-NAH-thah	pomegranate
granadilla	grah-nah-DEE-yah	passion fruit
granos	GRAH-nohs	grains
grasa	GRAH-sah	fat
grasa animal	GRAH-sah ah-nee-MAHL	butter
		lard

grasa de cerdo	GRAH-sah theh SEHR-doh	butter
		lard
grasa insaturada	GRAH-sah een-sah-too-RAH-thah	unsaturated fat
grasa monoinsaturada	GRAH-sah moh-noh-een-sah-tuh-RAH-thah	monounsaturated fat
grasa no saturada	GRAH-sah no sah-too-RAH-thah	unsaturated fat
grasa poliinsaturada	GRAH-sah poh-lee-een-sah-tuh-RAH-thah	polyunsaturated fat
grasa saturada	GRAH-sah sah-too-RAH-thah	saturated fat
guajolote	gwah-hoh-LOH-teh	turkey
guava	GWAH-bah	guava
guayaba/guayava	gwah-YAH-bah	guava
guineo	ghee-NEH-oh	banana
guisado	ghee-SAH-thoh	steak
guisado/a	ghee-SAH-thoh/thah	stewed
guisantes	ghee-SAHN-tehs	green peas

H

habichuelas	ah-bee-CHWEH-lahs	beans
habichuelas verdes	ah-bee-CHWEH-lahs behr-thehs	green beans
hambre	AHM-breh	hunger
hamburguesa	ahm-boor-GEH-sah	hamburger
harina	ah-REE-nah	flour
harina (de trigo) integral	ah-REE-nah (deh TREE-goh) een-teh-GRAHL	whole grain flour
harina de trigo	ah-REE-nah deh TREE-goh	wheat flour
heces sueltas	EH-sehs SWEHL-tahs	loose stools
helado	eh-LAH-thoh	ice cream
helado de agua	eh-LAH-thoh deh AH-gwah	sherbet/sorbet
helado de nieve	eh-LAH-thoh deh nee-eh-beh	sherbet/sorbet
hervido/a	ehr-BEE-thoh/thah	boiled
hierbas	YEHR-bahs	herbs
hierro	ee-EH-rroh	iron
hígado	EE-gah-thoh	liver
higo	EE-goh	fig

hiperglucemia	ee-pehr-gloo-SEH-mee-yah	hyperglycemia
hipoglucemia	ee-poh-gloo-SEH-mee-yah	hypoglycemia
hoja	OH-hah	cornhusk
hoja de maíz	OH-hah theh mah-EES	cornhusk
hongo	OHN-goh	mushroom
horneado/a	ohr-neh-AH-thoh/ah	baked
hot dog	HOHT dohg	hot dog
hotcakes	HOHT-kehks	pancakes
huevos	WEH-bohs	eggs
huevos revueltos	WEH-bohs rreh-BWEHL-tohs	eggs, scrambled

I

indigestion	een-dee-heh-stee-OHN	indigestion
integral	een-teh-GRAHL	whole grain
intolerancia a la lactosa	een-toh-leh-RAHN-see-ah ah lah lahk-TOH-sah	lactose intolerance

J

jalea	hah-LEH-yah	jelly
jamón	hah-MOHN	ham
jarabe	ha-RAH-beh	syrup
jícama	HEE-kah-mah	jicama
jitomate	hee-toh-MAH-teh	tomato
judías verdes	hoo-THEE-ahs BEHR-dehs	green beans
jueves	HWEH-behs	Thursday
jugo	HOO-goh	juice
jugo de arándano (agrio)	HOO-goh deh ah-RAHN-dah-noh (AH-gree-yoh)	cranberry juice
jugo de china	HOO-goh deh CHEE-nah	orange juice
jugo de frutas	HOO-goh deh FROO-tahs	fruit juice
jugo de jitomate	HOO-go deh hee-toh-MAH-teh	tomato juice
jugo de manzana	HOO-goh deh mahn-SAH-nah	apple juice
jugo de naranja	HOO-goh deh nah-RAHN-hah	orange juice
jugo de tomate	HOO-goh deh toh-MAH-teh	tomato juice

jugo de uva	HOO-goh deh OO-bah	grape juice
jugo de vegetales	HOO-goh deh beh-heh-TAH-lehs	vegetable juice
jugo de verduras	HOO-goh deh behr-DOO-rahs	vegetable juice

K

| *kiwi* | KEE-wee | kiwi |

L

lancet	lahn-SEH-tah	lancet
langosta	lahn-GOH-stah	lobster
leche	LEH-cheh	milk
leche achocolatada	LEH-cheh ah-choh-koh-lah-TAH-thah	chocolate milk
leche chocolate	LEH-cheh choh-koh-LAH-teh	chocolate milk
leche con Quik	LEH-cheh kohn KWEEK	chocolate milk
leche condensada	LEH-cheh kohn-dehn-SAH-thah	sweetened condensed milk
leche de chocolate	LEH-cheh deh choh-koh-LAH-teh	chocolate milk

leche de coco	LEH-cheh deh KOH-koh	coconut milk
leche de dos porciento	LEH-cheh deh dohs pohr-see-EHN-toh	reduced-fat (2%) milk
leche de un porciento	LEH-cheh deh oon pohr-see-EHN-toh	low-fat (1%) milk
leche descremada	LEH-cheh dehs-kreh-MAH-thah	low-fat milk nonfat (skim) milk
leche desgrasada	LEH-cheh-dehs-grah-SAH-thah	nonfat (skim) milk
leche en polvo	LEH-cheh ehn POHL-boh	powdered milk
leche entera	LEH-cheh ehn-TEH-rah	whole milk
leche evaporada	LEH-cheh eh-bah-poh-RAH-thah	evaporated milk
leche sin descremar	LEH-cheh seen dehs-kreh-MAHR	whole milk
leche sin grasa	LEH-cheh seen GRAH-sah	nonfat (skim) milk
lechuga	leh-CHOO-gah	lettuce
legumbres	leh-GOOM-brehs	legumes
lentejas	lehn-TEH-hahs	lentils
licuado	lee-KWAH-thoh	milkshake

lima	LEE-mah	lemon/lime
limón	lee-MOHN	lemon/lime
limonada	lee-moh-NAH-thah	lemonade
lonche	LOHN-cheh	lunch
lunes	LOOH-nehs	Monday

M

magdalena	mahg-dah-LEH-nah	cupcake
magnesio	mahg-NEH-see-oh	magnesium
maíz	mah-EES	corn
maizoro	mah-ee-SOH-roh	cereal
mal	mahl	bad
mandarina	mahn-dah-REE-nah	tangerine
mango	MAHN-goh	mango
maníes	mah-NEE-yehs	peanuts
manteca	mahn-TEH-kah	butter
		lard
manteca de maní	mahn-TEH-kah deh mah-NEE	peanut butter
mantecada	mahn-teh-KAH-thah	cupcake

mantecado	mahn-teh-KAH-thoh	ice cream
mantequilla	mahn-teh-KEE-yah	butter
		lard
mantequilla de cacahuate	mahn-teh-KEE-ya deh kah-kah-WAH-teh	peanut butter
mantequilla de maní	mahn-teh-KEE-ya deh mah-NEE	peanut butter
manzana	mahn-SAH-nah	apple
maracuyá	mah-rah-koo-YAH	passion fruit
marañones	mah-rahn-YOH-nes	cashews
margarina	mahr-gah-REE-nah	margarine
mariscos	mah-REE-skohs	shellfish
martes	MAHR-tehs	Tuesday
más	mahs	more
más o menos	mahs oh MEH-nohs	about (with time or numbers)
		around
masa	MAH-sah	corn-based dough for tamales or tortillas

mayonesa	mah-yoh-NEE-sah	mayonnaise
mazorca de maíz	mah-SOHR-kah deh mah-EES	corn on the cob
media	MEH-thee-ah	half
melocotón	meh-loh-koh-TOHN	peach
melón	meh-LOHN	cantaloupe
menos	MEH-nohs	less
merienda	meh-ree-EHN-dah	snack
mermelada	mehr-meh-LAH-thah	jelly
mezclar	mehs-KLAHR	mix
miel de abeja	mee-YEHL deh ah-BEH-hah	honey
miércoles	mee-YEHR-koh-lehs	Wednesday
mil	meel	one thousand
minerales	mee-neh-RAH-lehs	minerals
mitad	mee-TAHD	half
(con) moderación	(kohn) moh-deh-rah-see-OHN	(in) moderation
mole	MOH-leh	paste
		sauce
mollejas	moh-YEH-hahs	sweetbreads/gizzards

mollete	moh-YEH-teh	muffin
mora	MOH-rah	blackberry
mostaza	moh-STAH-sah	mustard
muffin	MOH-feen	muffin
muy	moo-wee	very

N

nabo	NAH-boh	turnip
naranja	nah-RAHN-hah	orange
nata	NAH-tah	cream
nauseas	NOW-see-ahs	nausea
nectarina	nehk-tah-REE-nah	nectarine
nieve	nee-EH-beh	ice cream
nopal	noh-PAHL	cactus
nopalitos	noh-pah-LEE-tohs	cactus
normalmente	nohr-mahl-MEHN-teh	normally
novecientos	noh-beh-see-EHN-tohs	nine hundred
noventa	noh-BEHN-tah	ninety
nueces	noo-EH-sehs	nuts
		pecans
		walnuts

nueces de Castilla	noo-EH-sehs deh kahs-TEE-yah	walnuts
nueces de nogal	noo-EH-sehs deh noh-GAHL	walnuts
nueve	noo-EH-beh	nine
nuez moscada	noo-EHS mohs-KAH-thah	nutmeg
nunca	NOON-kah	never
nutritivo/a	noo-tree-tee-boh/bah	nutritious

O

Oaxaca	wah-HAH-kah	white cheese made with cow's milk
obesidad	oh-beh-see-DAHD	obesity
ochenta	oh-CHEHN-tah	eighty
ocho	OH-choh	eight
ochocientos	oh-choh-see-EHN-tohs	eight hundred
oja	OH-hah	corn husk
once	OHN-seh	eleven
onza(s)	OHN-sah(s)	ounce(s)
orégano	oh-REH-gah-noh	oregano

orina	oh-REE-nah	urine
ostiones	oh-stee-OH-nehs	oysters

P

pacanas	pah-KAH-nahs	pecans
pai	PAH-ee	pie
palomitas (de maíz)	pah-loh-MEE-tahs (deh mah-EES)	popcorn
palta	PAHL-tah	avocado
pan	pahn	bread
pan blanco	pahn BLAHN-koh	white bread
pan blanco tostado	pahn BLAHN-koh toh-STAH-thoh	white toast
pan de trigo	pahn deh TREE-goh	wheat bread
pan de trigo tostado	pahn deh TREE-go toh-STAH-thoh	wheat toast
pan dulce	pahn DOOL-seh	pastry
pan integral	pahn een-teh-GRAHL	whole grain bread
pan integral tostado	pahn een-teh-GRAHL toh-STAH-thoh	whole grain toast

pan tostado	pahn toh-STAH-thoh	toast
panceta	pahn-SEH-tah	bacon
pancho	PAHN-choh	hot dog
páncreas	PAHN-kreh-ahs	pancreas
panecillo	pah-neh-SEE-yoh	bread roll
		muffin
panque	PAHN-keh	muffin
panquecas	pahn-KEH-kahs	pancakes
panqueques	pahn-KEH-kehs	pancakes
panques	PAHN-kehs	pancakes
papas	PAH-pahs	potatoes
papas doradas	PAH-pahs doh-rah-thahs	hash browns
papas fritas	PAH-pahs FREE-tahs	french fries
papaya	pah-PAH-yah	papaya
papitas	pah-PEE-tahs	french fries
papitas de bolsa	pah-PEE-tahs deh BOHL-sah	chips (snack chips)
papitas fritas	pah-PEE-tahs FREE-tahs	chips (snack chips)
parcha	PAHR-chah	passion fruit
pasas	PAH-sahs	prunes

pasas de uva	PAH-sahs deh OO-bah	prunes
pastel	pah-STEHL	cake
		pie
pastelillo	pahs-teh-LEE-yoh	cupcake
pastelito	pahs-teh-LEE-toh	cupcake
patatas	pah-TAH-tahs	potatoes
patilla	pah-TEE-yah	watermelon
pato	PAH-toh	duck
pavo	PAH-boh	turkey
pedacito(s)	peh-thah-SEE-toh(s)	small piece(s)
pedazo(s)	peh-THAH-soh(s)	piece(s)
pelar	peh-LAHR	peel (off)
pelón	peh-LOHN	nectarine
pepino	peh-PEE-noh	cucumber
pepitas	peh-PEE-tahs	pumpkin seeds
pera	PEH-rah	pear
perejil	peh-reh-HEEL	parsley
pescado	peh-SKAH-thoh	fish
petit pois	peh-tee PWAH	green peas
picada	pee-KAH-thah	barbecued meat

picadillo	pee-kah-DEE-yoh	hash (with meat)
picado/a	pee-KAH-thoh/thah	chopped
pie/pies	pee-EH/pee-EHS	feet/foot
piloncillo	pee-lohn-SEE-yoh	sugar, dark brown, unrefined
pimienta blanca	pee-mee-YEHN-tah BLAHN-kah	pepper (white)
pimienta negra	pee-mee-YEHN-tah NEH-grah	pepper (black)
pimiento dulce	pee-mee-EHN-toh DOOHL-seh	green bell pepper
pimiento verde	pee-mee-EHN-toh BEHR-deh	green bell pepper
pimientos rellenos	pee-mee-YEHN-tohs rreh-YEH-nohs	peppers, stuffed
piña	PEEN-yah	pineapple
pincelar asadera con aceite	peen-seh-LAHR ah-sah-THEH-rah kohn ah-see-EH-teh	brush (pan with oil)
piñones	peen-YOH-nehs	pine nuts
pipi	PEE-pee	urine

piraguas	pee-RAH-gwahs	shaved ice, with flavored syrup
pizza	PEET-sah	pizza
plátano	PLAH-tah-noh	banana
		plantain
plátano grande	PLAH-tah-noh GRAHN-deh	plantain
plátano macho	PLAH-tah-noh MAH-choh	plantain
plato principal	PLAH-toh preen-see-PAHL	main dish
pollo	POH-yoh	chicken
pomelo	poh-MEH-loh	grapefruit
popo	POH-poh	bowel movement/feces (informal)
porcentaje	pohr-sehn-TAH-heh	percentage
porciento	pohr-see-EHN-toh	percent
porción	pohr-see-OHN	portion
		serving size
porotos	poh-ROH-tohs	beans
porotos verdes	poh-ROH-tehs BEHR-dehs	green beans
postres	POHS-trehs	desserts

potasio	poh-TAH-see-oh	potassium
prenderse	prehn-DEHR-seh	latch on (for breastfeeding)
preparado/a	preh-pah-RAH-thoh/thah	prepared
presión (arterial) alta	preh-see-OHN (ahr-teh-ree-AHL) AHL-tah	high blood pressure
presión (arterial) baja	preh-see-OHN (ahr-teh-ree-AHL) BAH-hah	low blood pressure
prétzel	PREHT-sehl	pretzel
problemas al masticar	Proh-BLE-mahs ahl mahs-tee-KAHR	difficulty chewing
problemas al tragar	proh-BLE-mahs ahl trah-GAHR	difficulty swallowing
productos lácteos	proh-DOOK-tohs LAHK-teh-ohs	dairy
proteína	proh-teh-EE-nah	protein
pudin	poo-THEEN	pudding
puerco	PWEHR-koh	pork
puerro	PWEH-rroh	leek
pulpo	POOL-poh	octopus

Q

queso	KEH-soh	cheese
queso americano	KEH-soh ah-meh-ree-KAH-noh	American cheese
queso asadero	KEH-soh ah-sah-DEH-roh	white cheese made with cow's milk
queso azul	KEH-soh ah-SOOL	blue cheese
queso blanco	KEH-soh BLAHN-koh	white cheese
queso blanco grumoso	KEH-soh BLAHN-koh groo-MOH-soh	cottage cheese
queso cheddar	KEH-soh CHEH-thar	cheddar cheese
queso crema	KEH-soh KREH-mah	cream cheese
queso fresco	KEH-soh FREHS-koh	white cheese made with cow's milk
queso monterey jack	KEH-soh mohn-teh-reh JAHK	Monterey Jack cheese
queso mozzarella	KEH-soh moht-seh-REH-lah	mozzarella cheese
queso suizo	KEH-soh SWEE-soh	swiss cheese
quimbombó	keem-bohm-BOH	okra

quince	KEEN-she	fifteen
quingombó	keen-gohm-BOH	okra
quinientos	kee-nee-YEHN-tohs	five hundred
quínoa	KEEN-wah	quinoa

R

rábano	RRAH-bah-noh	radish
raciones	rrah-see-OH-nehs	portions
		servings
rallar	rrah-YAHR	grate
raspado	rrah-SPAH-thoh	shaved ice, with flavored syrup
rebanado/a	rreh-bah-NAH-thoh/thah	sliced
reducido en sodio	rreh-thoo-SEE-thoh ehn SOH-thee-oh	low-sodium
reflujo ácido	rreh-FLOO-hoh AH-see-thoh	heartburn/ acid reflux
refresco	rreh-FREHS-koh	soft drink
refresco de dieta	rreh-FREHS-koh deh dee-EH-tah	diet soft drink
refresco lite	rreh-FREHS-koh LAYT	diet soft drink

relleno/a	rreh-YEH-noh/nah	stuffed
remolacha	rreh-moh-LAH-chah	beet
repollitos de Bruselas	rreh-poh-YEE-tohs deh broo-SEH-lahs	brussels sprouts
repollo	rreh-POH-yoh	cabbage
requesón	rreh-keh-SOHN	cottage cheese
riñones	rreen-YOH-nehs	kidneys
rodaja	rroh-DAH-hah	slice
rosquillas	rroh-SKEE-yahs	donuts

S

sábado	SAH-bah-thoh	Saturday
sacaleche	sah-kah-LEH-cheh	breast pump
sal	sahl	salt
sal de ajo	sahl deh AH-hoh	garlic salt
salchicha	sahl-CHEE-chah	hot dog
		sausage
salsa	SAHL-sah	paste
		sauce
salsa de jitomate	SAHL-sah deh hee-toh-MAH-the	ketchup

salteado/a	sahl-teh-AH-thoh/thah	sautéed
		stir-fried
saludable	sah-loo-DAH-bleh	healthy
salvado	sahl-BAH-thoh	bran
sandía	sahn-DEE-yah	watermelon
sándwich	SAHND-weech	sandwich
sándwich de queso derretido	SAHND-weech deh KEH-soh deh-rreh-TEE-thoh	grilled cheese sandwich
sándwich de queso fundido	SAHND-weech deh KEH-soh foon-DEE-thoh	grilled cheese sandwich
sangre	SAHN-greh	blood
sano	SAH-noh	healthy
seco	SEH-koh	dry
sed	sehd	thirst
seis	SEH-ees	six
seiscientos	see-ehs-see-EHN-tohs	six hundred
selenio	seh-LEH-nee-oh	selenium
Señor	sehn-YOHR	Mr.
Señora	sehn-YOH-rah	Mrs.
Señorita	sehn-yoh-REE-tah	Miss
		Ms.

sequedad de vientre	seh-keh-THAD theh bee-EHN-treh	constipation
servido/a	sehr-BEE-thoh/thah	served
sesenta	seh-SEHN-tah	sixty
setecientos	seh-teh-see-EHN-tohs	seven hundred
setenta	seh-TEHN-tah	seventy
siempre	see-EHM-preh	always
siete	see-EH-teh	seven
sin	seen	without
sin azúcar	seen ah-SOO-kahr	sugar-free
sin grasa	seen GRAH-sah	fat-free
sin sal	seen sahl	salt-free
sirope	see-ROH-peh	syrup
sobrepeso	soh-breh-PEH-soh	overweight
soda	SOH-thah	soft drink
sodio	SOH-thee-oh	sodium
sofrito/a	soh-FREE-toh/thah	sautéed
		stir-fried
sopa	SOH-pah	soup
sorbete	sohr-BEH-teh	sherbet/sorbet

sueño	SWEHN-yoh	tired
suero	SWEH-roh	buttermilk

T

tajado/a	tah-HAH-thoh/thah	sliced
tarta	TAHR-tah	pie
taza(s)	TAH-sah(s)	cup(s)
tazas de medir	TAH-sahs deh meh-DEER	cup(s)
té	teh	tea
té frío	teh FREE-oh	iced tea
té helado	teh eh-LAH-thoh	iced tea
tira de ensayo	TEE-rah deh ehn-SAH-yoh	test strip
tira(s)	TEE-rah(s)	strip(s)
tocineta	toh-see-NEH-tah	bacon
tocino	toh-SEE-noh	bacon
tomate	toh-MAH-teh	tomato
tomatillo	toh-mah-TEE-yoh	tomatillo
toronja	toh-ROHN-hah	grapefruit
torreja	tohr-rreh-hah	french toast
torrija	tohr-rree-hah	french toast

torta	TOHR-tah	cake
		pie
		sandwich
tortilla	tohr-TEE-yah	tortilla
tortilla de harina	tohr-TEE-yah deh ah-REE-nah	flour tortilla
tortilla de huevo	tohr-TEE-ya deh WEH-boh	egg omelet
tortilla de maiz	tohr-TEE-yah deh mah-EES	corn tortilla
tortilla francesa	tohr-TEE-ya frahn-SEH-sah	egg omelet
tostada francesa	tohs-TAH-thah frahn-SEH-sah	french toast
tostadas	tohs-TAH-thahs	toast
tostaditas	toh-stah-THEE-tahs	chips (snack chips)
totopos	toh-TOH-pohs	chips (snack chips)
trastorno	trahs-TOHR-noh	disorder
trece	TREH-she	thirteen
treinta	TREHN-tah	thirty
tres	trehs	three
tres mil	trehs meel	three thousand

trescientos	trehs-see-EHN-tohs	three hundred
tripas	TREE-pahs	tripe
troceado	troh-seh-AH-thoh	chopped
trocito(s)	troh-SEE-toh(s)	small piece(s)
trozo(s)	TROH-soh(s)	piece(s)

U

uno	OO-noh	one
untado/a	oon-TAH-thoh/thah	spread
untar aceite al molde de hornear	uhn-TAHR ah-SEY-teh ahl MOHL-deh deh ohr-neh-AHR	brush (pan with oil)
usualmente	oo-soo-ahl-MEHN-teh	usually
uvas	OO-bahs	grapes
uvas pasas	OO-bahs PAH-sahs	raisins

V

v ocho	beh-oh-choh	vegetable juice
veinte	BEHN-the	twenty

verduras de hojas verdes	behr-DOO-rahs deh OH-hahs BEHR-dehs)	dark-green leafy vegetables
viernes	bee-YEHR-nehs	Friday
vino	BEE-noh	wine
vino blanco	BEE-noh BLAHN-koh	white wine
vino rojo	BEE-noh RROH-hoh	red wine
vino tinto	BEE-noh TEEN-toh	red wine
vitamina(s)	bee-tah-MEE-nah(s)	vitamin(s)
vómito(s)	BOH-mee-toh(s)	vomit

W

waffles	WAH-flehs	waffles
whiskey	güisqui, WEES-kee	whiskey

Y

yema de blanquillo	YEH-mah deh blahn-KEE-yoh	egg yolk
yema de huevo	YEH-mah deh WEH-boh	egg yolk
yogur	yoh-GOOR	yogurt

Additional Resources

Z

zanahorias	sah-nah-OH-ree-yahs	carrots
zapallito	sah-pah-YEE-toh	zucchini
zumo	THOO-moh	juice

Downloadable Food Cards

This edition of the *Academy of Nutrition and Dietetics Pocket Guide to Spanish for the Nutrition Professional,* Third Edition, comes with access to downloadable food cards. Professionals can print these full-color food cards and use them in client counseling and education.

You can find the downloadable food cards at www.eatrightstore.org/PGtoSpanish3e-Downloads.

Most serving sizes provided on the food cards are food group amounts designated by MyPlate.gov as equivalent to 1 cup or 1 oz. Protein foods (meat, poultry, and seafood) are presented as typical portions with the equivalent weight included. For foods that are not included in MyPlate, the serving size is the Food and Drug Administration Reference Amout Commonly Consumed (RACC) per eating occasion.

Continuing Professional Education

This edition of *Academy of Nutrition and Dietetics Pocket Guide to Spanish for the Nutrition Professional*, Third Edition, offers readers 3 hours of Continuing Professional Education (CPE) credit.

Readers may earn credit by completing the interactive online quiz at: https://publications.webauthor.com/PG_to_Spanish_3e.